Understanding Trauma and Dissociation

A GUIDE FOR THERAPISTS, PATIENTS AND LOVED ONES

Lynn Mary Karjala, Ph.D.

Psychology Innovations Press

Understanding Trauma and Dissociation: A Guide for Therapists, Patients and Loved Ones by Lynn Mary Karjala, Ph.D.

Second Revised Edition

ISBN: 978-0-9984545-0-4 (paperback)
ISBN: 987-0-9984545-2-8 (ebook)

Psychology Innovations Press
Roswell, Georgia
www.karjala.com

Quantity sales. Special discounts are available on quantity purchases by corporations, associations, and others. For details, contact the "Special Sales Department" at the address above.

Cover design by Mila | milabookcovers.com
Interior design by Amit Dey | amitdey2528@gmail.com

Quintessential Safe Place imagery reprinted by permission from Heartland Initiative, Inc.

Publisher's Cataloging-In-Publication Data
(Prepared by The Donohue Group, Inc.)

Names: Karjala, Lynn Mary, author.
Title:Understanding trauma and dissociation : a guide for therapists, patients and loved ones / Lynn Mary Karjala, Ph.D.
Description: [2nd edition]. | Roswell, Georgia : Psychology Innovations Press, [2023] | Previously published: Atlanta, GA : ThomasMax Pub., 2007.
Identifiers: ISBN: 978-0-9984545-0-4 (paperback) | 987-0-9984545-2-8 (ebook)
Subjects: LCSH: Dissociative disorders. | Traumatic neuroses. | Psychic trauma--Alternative treatment. | Memory--Psychological aspects. | Mind and body therapies. | Energy psychology. | LCGFT: Self-help publications. | BISAC: PSYCHOLOGY / Psychopathology / Post-Traumatic Stress Disorder (PTSD) | PSYCHOLOGY / Psychotherapy / Counseling. | HEALTH & FITNESS / Alternative Therapies.
Classification: LCC: RC553.D5 K3 2023 | DDC: 616.8521--dc23

This book is dedicated to my teachers:
to the many clinicians and researchers who have
helped to guide my footsteps and shape
my understanding of this work,
and to my patients,
who have been the greatest teachers of all.

Table of Contents

Author's Note

Many style manuals these days allow the use of the pronoun "they" to refer to a single person—for example, "Before a child can run, they have to learn to walk." In a book about people who have many dissociated parts, however, referring to the core person as "they" could be very confusing. As a result, I've chosen in many instances to stay with singular pronouns, alternating them somewhat randomly. In addition, the majority of patients who are identified with childhood abuse and dissociative disorders are female. In the chapters on trauma and treatment, for that reason, I most often refer to a patient as "she." It's important to remember, however, that there certainly are others with these same issues and that the principles and techniques described here apply equally well to all genders.

Disclaimer

Many of the clinical examples described in this book are real or based on real events. The names of the people involved, however, are entirely fictitious.

Some of the material for this work was adapted from Dr. Karjala's second book, *Healing Everyday Traumas: Free Yourself from the Scars of Bullying, Criticism and Other Old Wounds.*

This book is designed to provide information about the subject matter covered. It is sold with the understanding that the publisher and author are not engaged in rendering psychological or other professional services to its readers. If psychological or other expert assistance is required, the services of a competent professional should be sought.

Although every effort has been made to verify the accuracy of the information contained herein, the author and publisher assume no responsibility for any errors or omissions. The purpose of this book is to educate and inform. The author and publisher shall have neither liability nor responsibility to any person or entity with respect to any loss or damage caused or alleged to be caused directly or indirectly by the information contained in this book.

CHAPTER 1

Introduction

Dissociation is a very common mental mechanism, and most people have experienced it in some form. For example, if you've ever driven along a familiar route, arrived at your destination, and then found that you couldn't remember a good chunk of the trip, you've experienced dissociation. The same is true if you've ever become so absorbed in a book or movie that you "saw" yourself in the scene of the story and became unaware of your surroundings. Or if you've been listening to someone talk and suddenly realized that you hadn't heard what he or she was saying. Or perhaps you've had an experience in which you did or said something, knew that you had done or said it, but had a persistent feeling that this behavior was "not me" or "not like me." These are forms of dissociation that people commonly experience every day.

Dissociation is also a defense mechanism—that is, a technique the human mind uses to protect itself from thoughts, feelings or experiences that are painful or disturbing. There are many different defense mechanisms, and virtually everyone uses them.

For the most part, defense mechanisms are subconscious—that is, we're not aware that we're using them. They have to be in order to do their job of keeping painful material out of our conscious thoughts. Once you start to become aware of a particular defense mechanism, it's already breaking down, and you also start to become aware of some or all of what's behind it.

The term "defense mechanism" has taken on a distinctly negative connotation over the years, almost as if we should all be ashamed of having or using them. For that reason, psychotherapists often refer to them today as coping mechanisms, because that puts our attention on their positive purpose: they exist in order to help us cope with aspects of our experience that are disturbing, painful and overwhelming.

As with most things in life, however, there's a cost associated with this benefit. Every defense mechanism distorts reality in some way—that's how it works. The more heavily we rely on these mechanisms in general, the more our reality becomes distorted. And the more we rely on just one or two to the exclusion of other methods of coping, the more likely the defense mechanism itself will become an increasingly serious problem, causing significant interference in our social relationships, occupational functioning, and other aspects of daily life. You might think that using many defense mechanisms would make you "sicker" than using just one, but that's not the case. Having a wide repertoire of coping techniques available to you gives you more flexibility in responding to difficult situations and makes it more likely that you'll be able to respond in healthy, adaptive ways.

The purpose of this book is to help you understand the ins and outs of dissociation, both as a positive coping mechanism and as the cause of various kinds of disorders. Chapter 2 explains in greater depth what dissociation is and how it relates to other kinds of coping mechanisms. It includes ideas about how and why dissociation develops and why some people have a much higher dissociative ability than others. Chapter 3 discusses the differences between traumatic and nontraumatic memories and an important theory about the origins and consequences of those differences. Chapter 4 describes different levels of dissociation and the kinds of disorders that can arise as a person's use of dissociation becomes more extensive.

Chapters 5 and 6 focus on the most extreme form of dissociation, which is now known as Dissociative Identity Disorder, or DID. This is the condition that used to be called Multiple Personality Disorder, or MPD. As you'll see in this chapter, the change of name was not merely cosmetic. Rather, it reflects a different way of thinking about dissociative disorders, one that I've found enormously helpful in my work as a therapist.

By looking at dissociation in its most extreme form, we'll be able to see and understand dissociative phenomena more clearly. However, it's important to remember that we all use dissociation. We all have parts or aspects of ourselves that perform certain roles and functions. In fact, we have many of the same kinds of parts and aspects that people with DID do. By understanding how the parts function in a DID system, where they're more distinct and obvious, we'll also be able to recognize the same functions in their more subtle forms as they occur in the rest of us.

Chapter 7 discusses the treatment of trauma and the dissociative disorders. We'll look at the three-phase model, considered the standard of care in trauma treatment. Within the three phases of containment and stabilization, memory processing, and self and relational development, there's a variety of excellent visualization tools that can further the process of therapy. Several of those tools are described in detail in Chapters 8, 9, 10, and 11. Chapter 12 discusses some of the new, alternative techniques from the field of mind-body medicine. Chapter 13 introduces you to a few of these tools. In my experience, these powerful new techniques — especially when combined with good, traditional therapy — can significantly enhance the effectiveness of the therapeutic process. Again, it's important to note that all of these tools, both conventional and alternative, work just as well with patients who have lesser degrees of trauma as they do with patients who have DID. Lastly, I've included an appendix on the science of trauma for readers who want to have a deeper understanding of the impact of trauma on neurological and physiological levels.

My main goal as I wrote this book was to make the material both readable and interesting for a wide variety of people, from the nonprofessional person who knows little or nothing about dissociation to the therapist with years of experience. For patients and their loved ones who are struggling with dissociative issues and the problems — even the havoc — they can cause, my aim is to give you a framework that will allow you to understand these phenomena in a more positive light and begin to deal with them more effectively. For the therapist, whether you're just starting out or have been in the field for quite a while, I've included details and examples from my own work that may give you a fresh perspective. (Most of what I know about dissociative disorders I *didn't* learn in grad school.) They may also give you new and different ways of talking about these areas with your patients or clients. Indeed, my dream as I write this book is that therapists and patients, or patients and loved ones, will read the book together, so that they have a common language for understanding and communicating with each other in deeper and better ways. For every reader at every level, my ultimate hope is to give you hope — that the potential does exist for these problems to be resolved and healed.

CHAPTER 2

The Nature and Origin of Dissociation

As I mentioned in Chapter 1, dissociation is a defense (or coping) mechanism. Essentially, it's the ability of the human mind to take an experience, split it into different pieces, and act on those pieces separately from each other. One type of split you might think of as horizontal—the different pieces are simply put in separate compartments in your conscious mind. You're aware of both pieces, but you don't tend to think of them at the same time. Another type of split might be called vertical—one or more aspects of the experience stay conscious, or at least available to your conscious mind, while other aspects are kept subconscious and out of your awareness. You might think of amnesia as the most extreme form of vertical dissociation. We'll discuss that in more detail in a later chapter.

Dissociation is an early, primitive defense mechanism; there is evidence that the capacity to dissociate is inborn, hardwired into the brain. When I first began to study trauma and dissociation intensively, I started seeing them everywhere. So much so, in fact, that I thought I must be overdiagnosing—just as when you first learn about a particular mental illness and are immediately sure that that's what you've got. (Or if not you, then certainly all of your friends!) As I continued to work, though, I concluded that my original impression was correct— they *are* everywhere. Since then, I've come to believe that virtually all psychological disorders are trauma-related. The exceptions would be those that are caused by physical damage to the brain, such as Alzheimer's, and those that have a biochemical component, which may include schizophrenia and bipolar disorder. I've also come to believe that dissociation is *the* original defense mechanism and that all of the other defenses are based on it in one way or another. To illustrate this point, let's look at some examples of other defense mechanisms, as they've traditionally been described

Denial is another primitive defense, meaning that it doesn't rely on the more sophisticated, mature functions of the brain to work. It happens when there's some aspect of the external world that's simply too painful for us to face, so we can't allow ourselves to see it. The classic example is the alcoholic who admits that he drinks but vehemently denies that he has a drinking problem, in spite of the mounting evidence that's increasingly apparent to people around him. He's not knowingly lying when he says he doesn't have a problem—he's genuinely unaware of it. In other words, he's kept the knowledge of his behavior in his conscious awareness—he knows that he drinks—but he's dissociated the significance and the danger of the behavior.

As an aside, some alcoholics experience what are called blackouts as a result of drinking. While having a blackout, the person acts and talks almost normally, but he has no memory, no conscious knowledge, of his behavior afterward. I have a hypothesis that blackouts may only happen to those who also have high dissociative ability and that they're actually some form of dissociative phenomenon.

Another, more poignant example of denial is one we sometimes see in women who've been raped or assaulted. Some of these women begin to engage in risky behavior, such as walking down dark alleys at night, and a percentage of them do wind up getting assaulted again. It's certainly not that they're "asking for it" on any level — actually, it's exactly the opposite of that. These women are so terrified and overwhelmed by the sense of danger that they dissociate it. They don't feel it at all. At most, they might feel vaguely uneasy, but they talk themselves out of it by telling themselves that they're just being silly. The dissociation makes them unable to see danger cues that other people would readily pick up on.

Repression is similar to denial, except that it's the person's internal experience — thoughts or feelings — rather than external reality that's the source of the distress. A woman who hates her mother, but who also believes that one must honor one's parents in order to be a good person, is caught in a terrible conflict. One way for her to deal with this conflict is to repress the unacceptable feelings, which means that she doesn't allow them into her conscious awareness. It's easy to see this as another example of vertical dissociation: her belief about honoring one's parents remains conscious, while her feelings of hatred are dissociated and subconscious.

Reaction formation might be seen as a variation of repression. In this case, the person not only buries the unacceptable feelings but displays the opposite, often in an exaggerated way. The woman in the previous example might loudly praise her mother as a saint and exhaust herself in waiting on her.

The defense mechanism called **isolation** isn't what it sounds like. It doesn't refer to a person who is cutting himself off from social contacts. In the traditional psychiatric definition, isolation is the cutting off of cognition (thinking) from affect (feeling). If you've ever talked with someone who had just received a life-threatening diagnosis, you may have seen this defense in action. A person who has just learned that he has cancer may talk about the disease as calmly and unemotionally as if he were discussing the grocery list. The knowledge is there, but the feelings are simply gone — they've been dissociated and stored on a subconscious level. This mechanism protects the person, at least temporarily, from the overwhelming fear, anxiety, sadness and even guilt that hearing the diagnosis of cancer can arouse.

Compartmentalization is a good example of what I called horizontal dissociation. This defense is similar to isolation, except that both sides of the conflict remain available to your conscious mind. They're simply not allowed to meet. In my younger days, I smoked for over 20 years. The dangers of smoking may not have been widely known when I started, but they'd certainly been well publicized long before I quit. Like many other smokers, I handled the conflict by keeping the two cognitions, "I am a smoker" and "smoking is dangerous," compartmentalized and dissociated from each other as much as possible. **Rationalization** is a more sophisticated type of defense mechanism. In this case, the person goes beyond simple denial or repression and uses logic to come up with reasons to justify unacceptable feelings or behaviors. For instance, a man whose father was verbally abusive holds deep anger toward him and doesn't want to see him. But he justifies not wanting to go for a visit by saying that it's too far, it's too expensive, he can't take the time off work, the kids are in school, etc. All of those things may be true, but the real reason he doesn't want to make the trip has been dissociated.

These are only a few examples, but they illustrate the point that defense mechanisms—as they've traditionally been described—can all be seen, in one way or another, as variations on a theme. Dissociation seems to be the engine that makes them run.

As I mentioned earlier, the ability to dissociate appears to be inborn, a natural quality of the human brain, and everyone has at least some level of this ability. It's clear, however, that some people are able to use dissociation to a much greater extent than most of us can achieve. For example, one of my patients told me that he never needed anesthesia for routine dental procedures such as fillings. Just before the dentist started to work, Dan would use his dissociative talent to "travel" to a beach on a Caribbean island. He would bask in the sun in complete comfort until the dentist indicated that he was finished.

What causes the differences in ability? As with all forms of talent, the answer is a combination of nature and nurture, of genetic inheritance and learning from experience. To become a concert pianist, you have to have a high level of musical talent, you have to start your training early, and you have to practice, practice, practice. If you don't start playing until you're 10 or 12, you may be good, but it's very unlikely that you'll ever reach a virtuoso level. The same is true of dissociative talent. The highest dissociators are those who have a strong talent *and* who had reasons to exercise that talent early and often. That's why virtually all people with Dissociative Identity Disorder turn out to have a history of severe and prolonged childhood abuse or neglect. If a person doesn't have this disorder by about age 7, it's very unlikely that he ever will.

Why age 7? In the early 20th century, psychologist Jean Piaget made what was then a startling discovery: children don't think like adults. It's not just that they have less knowledge about the world. It's that their understanding of the world is qualitatively different. (I won't go into all of the details of Piaget's work here, just a few highlights.) Beginning at about age 2, in what Piaget called the preoperational stage, children begin to be able to think symbolically. They can use words to represent objects that aren't present or to describe an action without performing it. They can sit in a cardboard box and pretend that it's a racecar. But it's not until around age 7, when they develop what Piaget called concrete operations, that they become able to understand elementary logic. Among other things, they begin to understand cause and effect. They also come to realize that other people have different perspectives, both literally (we look at the same object from different angles) and figuratively (we have different thoughts and feelings about something). It's these kinds of abilities that allow us to begin using the higher-level defense mechanisms, such as rationalization. In any kind of situation, people typically rely on their most advanced skills first, only resorting to primitive ones if the more sophisticated ones don't work. As we become more mature, then, we tend to rely less and less on the primitive defense mechanisms such as dissociation—unless early trauma has made it a fixture.

By the way, the ages at which these changes occur may differ across different cultures, but the stages described by Piaget have found to be quite consistent around the world.

You might be starting to wonder how much you yourself dissociate. How might you be using dissociation or other coping mechanisms? Don't be surprised, though, if this question is a bit difficult to answer at this point. These mechanisms aren't always easy to recognize in ourselves. Indeed, if you can see that you've been using a particular defense mechanism, it's already beginning to break down. A man who realizes that he's been in denial about how much he's been drinking, for example, is no longer fully in denial. (He may still be denying that his drinking has caused any real problems.) But imagine yourself dropping a pebble into a pond. Long after the pebble drops out of sight, you can still see the ripples in the water. In the same way, even when we don't know what the original issue is, we can often take a pretty good guess by noticing the *effects* that it created. In the next two chapters, we'll talk about some of the effects that dissociation—and the other defense mechanisms—can cause.

CHAPTER 3

Traumatic vs. Nontraumatic Memory

For a long time, there was a great deal of controversy
about the nature of traumatic memory and, in particular,
whether traumatic memories are different from "normal"
memories. On an experiential level, trauma survivors
consistently tell us their traumatic memories *feel* different.
They don't feel like long-ago, faraway events, but rather like
experiences that are happening, at full intensity, right now
in the present moment. There is also an increasing body of
research indicating that traumatic events trigger responses
in the central nervous system (especially the limbic system)
and in the endocrine system that don't happen in response
to nontraumatic events. It's been speculated that these
biochemical and physiological responses create long-term,
perhaps even permanent, changes in neuronal pathways
in the brain.

I touch on some of the research findings in this chapter.
For readers who are interested in going more deeply into

this subject, I've included an appendix on "The Science of Trauma." It provides a more thorough explanation of how traumatic experiences trigger a specific sequence of physiological changes in the body. It also discusses studies of the neurological and physiological changes that help us understand why trauma is experienced as it is.

For the nonprofessional reader who doesn't want or need to go into that much detail, the following is a theory that has been influential in the thinking of many clinicians, especially those working on the front lines of trauma treatment. It focuses on the psychological or experiential differences between traumatic and nontraumatic memory.

The BASK Model of Experience

This theory suggests that our memory of any experience we've had is made up of four major components that form the acronym BASK (Braun, 1988). "B" stands for behavior. This includes all of the body movements that we made or witnessed during the experience. "A" stands for affect, another word for emotion. In a pleasant memory, this might include happiness, joy, excitement and love. In a traumatic experience, it's likely to be fear, anxiety, anger, rage, guilt, shame, hopelessness, helplessness. "S" is for sensation, all the sensory information that gets registered during the experience — sights, sounds, smells, pain, etc. "K" stands for knowledge, the cognitive awareness of what happened, including our interpretations of the event and the beliefs we form about it.

In nontraumatic circumstances, these four components flow along together. We may not be equally aware of all of them all the time, but we *can* be aware of them if we turn our attention to them. For example, you can choose to be aware right now of what you're doing, what you're feeling, what you're thinking, and what body sensations are being registered. Then all of the components are stored together in normal narrative memory.

Normal storage is like leaving the memory out in the yard exposed to the elements. Parts of it, especially the sensory information, erode very quickly, so that when we recall it there's a clear difference between experiencing it the first time and remembering it afterwards.

Traumatic Dissociation

However, something very different seems to happen when people are under massive stress. The theory suggests that, during a trauma, the various BASK components of the experience may become dissociated or split off from each other and stored separately. There are three very important consequences that we can observe from this splitting off.

The first consequence is that the person may be unable to recall one or more of the components — the **B**ehaviors, **A**ffect, **S**ensations or **K**nowledge — of the experience. She may even have complete amnesia for the event — in other words, all four of the components may be dissociated.

The second consequence is that the experience is not exposed to the normal weathering that occurs with nontraumatic memories. It's as if a part of the mind is frozen in time. Peripheral details may become lost or distorted, but the central part of the memory is almost perfectly preserved. According to the theory, this is why the memory retains all of the emotional impact of the original event, and even the physical sensations. If it does get recalled to consciousness, the person feels as if she's *reliving* it, not simply remembering it.

It's worth noting that the amount of time doesn't seem to matter at all. The Roman philosopher Publius Terentius Afer is credited with originating the expression, "Time heals all wounds." He said a few other things that were more apt, but in this case he was completely wrong. The passage of time may cover up emotional wounds but, just by itself, it does not heal them. Even decades later, the traumatic experience may be just as powerful as the day it happened.

However, there is a major difference between physical objects literally frozen in ice and memories "frozen" in time. An object frozen in ice is inert—that is, it has no perceptible effect on anything around it. That's not true of traumatic memories. Even though some or all of the components of the memories are dissociated and we may not even be able to recall them on a conscious level, they can still exert insidious effects on our present-day behavior and experiences.

The third consequence is that some or all of the components may intrude into the person's ongoing experience, in the form of flashbacks. Essentially, a flashback is the sudden return, or un-dissociation, of a dissociated memory or memory component.

Flashbacks come in assorted shapes and sizes. Many people associate the term "flashback" with the picture of the military vet crouching in the garden thinking he's back on the battlefield. It does sometimes happen that the whole experience floods the mind all at once, to the point that it overwhelms our awareness of where we are here and now, and we actually behave as if we were back in that other time and place.

However, that dramatic, stereotypical kind of flashback actually seems to be fairly rare compared to the other types. Much more commonly reported are flashbacks of just one or two of the BASK components at a time. For example, many people report that they've had an intense feeling of sadness, fear or anger that they know has little or no connection to the present moment. Or the feeling tone may be appropriate to the current situation, but the magnitude of it is clearly way out of proportion. The odds are that they're experiencing an affective flashback, a surge of emotion from some earlier event, but without the knowledge component that would help them make sense of it.

Another example is what are called "body memories." A body memory is a flashback of the sensation component of an experience. A patient called me one morning very upset because she had woken up during the night with the distinct sensation of a hand grasping her ankle. It was so real and complete that she threw the covers back to look, even though she knew she was alone in the room. This turned out to be the first clue to a previously unknown trauma: we later discovered that she had been attacked and held down when she was a child, and this was a vivid re-experiencing of one small piece of that incident.

That particular example also illustrates the fact that flashbacks can occur during sleep, as nightmares. It's very unlikely that we would find all nightmares to be flashbacks. In fact, there's some evidence that the majority of our dreams—perhaps as high as 60 or 70 percent—are negative in tone. But a small proportion of dreams take the form of recurring nightmares—that is, nightmares that the person experiences more than once and that are almost identical each time. My clinical experience has led me to conclude that most, perhaps all, recurring nightmares are flashbacks of actual events, or that they at least contain flashback elements.

Healing a traumatic memory involves transforming it into a normal, narrative memory. Following Braun's theory, the objective of therapy was to resolve the trauma by un-dissociating and reintegrating the BASK components of the experience in the person's conscious awareness of the present moment. We'll discuss the process of treatment in much greater detail starting in Chapter 7.

Consequences of Increasing Dissociation

Children get hurt. Some are hurt in extreme ways, such as physical or sexual abuse; but all of us have been hurt one way or another. No one gets through childhood without experiencing teasing, ridicule or even being punched or shoved. My second book, *Healing Everyday Traumas* (2022), talks about these more commonplace forms of abuse and their effects.

Psychologist Jim Dillon (2001) pointed out that children are completely alive to their own feelings until they encounter what he calls "pollutants" such as bullying and put-downs. These pollutants then cause them to deny their feelings and dissociate, or split off, parts of themselves.

Denial and dissociation are indeed common and very early defense mechanisms. But children also begin to deny their feelings because they're actively taught to do so. How many times have you heard a parent say, "Oh, that's just a little scrape — why are you making such a big deal out of it?" "Big boys don't cry." And all of us learned that "sticks and stones may break my bones, but names can never hurt me." I've often wondered where that particular gem of wisdom came from — of course it hurts when someone calls you a name, especially if you're a child whose feelings are still alive. But if the child shows those feelings, he gets called a crybaby or a sissy — causing more hurt on top of the original insult. In response, children begin to dissociate and bury more and more of their feelings.

Abusers are often quite good at teaching children to distort their own reality. Perhaps the parent or older sibling says, "Quit your crying — that didn't hurt!" The child's experience was that it did hurt — a lot — but, being a child, he usually assumes that adults know better than he does. So he allows the adult's definition of the situation to override his own perception. He tells himself, "Okay, I thought that was what 'hurt' meant, but I guess not. I'm really confused. I must be really stupid." The child may not be able to articulate the thought quite as clearly as that, but the meaning registers nonetheless.

The pain and confusion and self-blame and anger continue to build. And we keep shoving them under the rug because we're taught that's what good people do. Our feelings get deader and more disconnected. Dissociation is not a fine-tipped artist's brush; it's more like a street sweeper's push broom. When it comes to dissociation, finesse is not where it's at. Anything connected with the dissociated event, anything that might break down the dissociative boundary and cause the memory or feeling to return, is also dissociated. This may even include happy memories, if they serve as triggers for traumatic memories. For example, Sharon dearly cherished her memory of the one time her mother smiled at her and said "Good job!" But she couldn't allow herself to think about it, much less feel how good it felt, because it was the only time. Thinking about it immediately gave rise to a flood of feeling about all the times her mother could have said it and didn't, all the ways her mother let her know that she wasn't good enough.

But painful feelings don't simply go away when we dissociate them. In fact, with repeated exposure to the same kinds of experiences, the feelings develop into traumatic patterns or themes. Then we begin to generate beliefs about our experiences. The human mind doesn't simply observe; it automatically interprets, draws conclusions, attempts to make sense of what it observes. One instance of feeling stupid may pass us by, but "I feel stupid," if repeated over and over, soon becomes "I *am* stupid."

So the traumatic feelings and their resulting beliefs continue to accumulate. Like deadly carbon monoxide coming from a defective space heater, we don't see these things directly, but they can affect us strongly. Sometimes the consequences are merely inconvenient, but sometimes they can be disastrous.

No one with dissociated trauma is completely symptom-free. Even with "normal" levels of dissociation, eventually the fear or anger or guilt starts coming out sideways. Wounded people often behave in self-defeating or self-centered ways. Ann's self-esteem takes a beating, and she becomes overly critical of herself and others, pushing people away with her judgmental attitude. John runs red lights as if the rules of the road don't apply to him. Henry ridicules his wife for being overweight and, when she objects, he tells her she's "oversensitive" and can't take a joke. He never apologizes for anything; when something goes wrong, it's always someone else's fault.

As the pain and anger continue to accumulate, dissociated and unprocessed, the problems become more intense. Louise gets into a series of destructive relationships. John explodes at work. Susan becomes bitingly sarcastic and sabotages her team's efforts. Jim's blood pressure goes sky-high. George's road rage is so bad that he fantasizes about running someone off the road and nearly does it. And some kid in Colorado or Kentucky or Georgia picks up a gun and brings it to school with murderous intent.

The earlier, the more frequent, and the more intense the dissociation, the more likely it is the person will develop a dissociative disorder, with all its complications and difficulties. We'll discuss the range of those disorders in the next chapter.

CHAPTER 4

The Dissociative Disorders

A s I mentioned in Chapter 1, dissociation is a normal and probably universal phenomenon. There are many kinds of dissociation that are entirely benign. To return to an example from that discussion, you've probably had the experience at least once of driving over a familiar route, arriving at your destination, and finding that you couldn't remember anything about the drive. You must have driven reasonably safely and appropriately, because even a honk from a car horn would most likely have shaken you out of your reverie. So part of you must have been attending to the road, even while the other part was...somewhere else.

However, the more we rely on dissociation—or any single defense mechanism, for that matter—the more likely it is that the defense mechanism itself will become a serious problem. Think of it like a leg cast: it's wonderfully helpful when you need it, but you wouldn't want to live in it permanently. The point at which a coping mechanism begins to cause more problems than it solves is when it becomes a disorder rather than a help. There are several types of dissociative disorder that have been recognized and described.

Dissociative Amnesia

According to the American Psychiatric Association's *Diagnostic and Statistical Manual, 5th ed., text rev.* (2022, also known as the DSM-5 TR), amnesia is the inability to recall one or more chunks of important autobiographical information. It's not the same thing as simple forgetting. The amount of information is more extensive than can be accounted for by normal processes, and the type of information that's lost is more distinctively personal. To use a lighthearted example, it's probably normal forgetting if I can't recall the name of someone I just met, but it's not a good sign if I can't remember my own.

Memory loss can be caused by a number of factors, including brain injury, seizure disorders, substance abuse, and dementia. What distinguishes dissociative amnesia, however, is that it's not related to any form of physical brain damage or deterioration. And whereas the memory loss caused by brain damage is often permanent, dissociative amnesia is reversible.

Dissociative amnesia is caused by severe stress or trauma, and the information that's lost is related in some way to the trauma. The most common form is called localized amnesia, in which the person is unable to recall anything that happened within a particular time period. In selective amnesia, the person can recall some aspects of the events during the specific time period but not others.

The most severe form is generalized, or global, amnesia, in which the person is unable to recall any personal information, any details of her previous life.

The traumatic origins of dissociative amnesia show up in the fact that it's only personally significant information that's lost, not impersonal information. Even in generalized amnesia, the individual doesn't lose the knowledge of his native language, basic arithmetic, or the usual customs of his culture. When an area of knowledge or skill is lost, it's because it's *related* to the trauma in some way.

Post-Traumatic Stress Disorder

After people have experienced a severe trauma, they often experience and display a particular pattern of symptoms. This pattern of symptoms is called Post-Traumatic Stress Disorder, or PTSD. Although PTSD is officially classified as an anxiety disorder, it's characterized by significant dissociative symptoms.

As described in the DSM-5 TR, one set of PTSD symptoms involves **re-experiencing the trauma** in one or more ways. Distressing thoughts, feelings, and images of the traumatic event may intrude into the person's everyday awareness. It's common to have nightmares of the event. The person may at times feel or act as if the event were happening again in the present. And people often experience both intense psychological pain and symptoms of physical distress (e.g., sweating, shaking) whenever they encounter something that brings up the memory of the event.

A second set of symptoms has to do with **avoidance behavior**. People who have been traumatized often go to great lengths to avoid anything that might remind them of the trauma (and therefore cause the kind of re-experiencing just described). They avoid thinking or talking about the event. They avoid objects, activities, places and people that are associated with the event in any way.

A third set of symptoms includes **negative feelings and beliefs** that arise out of the trauma. The repercussions of the trauma don't end when the event does. Some negative emotions, such as terror or shame, may have been experienced by the person during the trauma itself (and may continue afterward), but additional feelings such as guilt and self-loathing may arise in the aftermath. It's very common for negative beliefs to develop as a result of the trauma as well. These beliefs may include such things as irrational self-blame, survivor guilt ("I didn't deserve to survive"), a sense of being permanently damaged, or a judgment that no one can be trusted.

Included in this third category of negatively altered cognitions and mood is a general emotional numbness and the dissociation of emotional responses. Traumatized people have trouble showing or even experiencing positive emotions such as love, joy, excitement, or enthusiasm. They often feel detached from the people and things they cared deeply about before the trauma. They may drift away from activities that used to be important to them. They may be unable to recall important aspects of the event—or even the event as a whole. And they may have little or no hope that their lives will ever be back to normal.

A fourth set of symptoms includes various forms of **physiological arousal**. These include insomnia, irritability, anger outbursts, difficulty concentrating, and an exaggerated startle response. One of the classic symptoms in this category is hypervigilance, the intent scanning for any hint of threat or danger. In fact, psychologist Judith Herman (1992) suggested the hallmark of PTSD is the constant alternation between two specific states. One is a state of being numb, "zoned out" and dissociated, and the other state is being hypervigilant and hyperalert.

Acute Stress Reaction

PTSD can't officially be diagnosed until the symptoms have persisted at least 30 days after the traumatic event. Within the first 30 days, the appropriate diagnosis is acute stress reaction. The pattern of symptoms is almost identical to PTSD, but there are some differences. In particular, the dissociative symptoms of numbness, detachment, and lack of emotional responsiveness may be much more prominent, obvious even to an untrained observer. There may also be more intense or frequent episodes of derealization or depersonalization. In derealization, the external world — even very familiar surroundings — seems unreal, unfamiliar, or dream-like. In depersonalization, the normal sense of self is seriously impaired. The person feels detached from her own mental or physical being, as if she's observing someone else's thoughts or actions.

Dissociative Identity Disorder

Dissociative Identity Disorder, or DID, is the most severe form of dissociative disorder. Briefly, it's characterized by two or more distinct personality states that are capable of taking executive control of the body. The feature that distinguishes DID from the other disorders in this category is that at least one of these personality states has amnesia for the thoughts and actions of one or more of the other personality states. We'll discuss DID at much greater length in the next chapter.

Dissociative Disorder Not Otherwise Specified

Dissociative Disorder Not Otherwise Specified, or DDNOS, is a catch-all for any form of dissociative disorder that doesn't fit in any of the other categories. One of the most common forms of DDNOS, however, has almost all of the symptoms of DID. The major difference between this disorder and DID is that there's no amnesia among the personality states. Each one can remember what the other ones did, said, or thought, although they may not share each other's beliefs or feelings.

Diagnosing Dissociative Disorders

If you're a patient or loved one, you probably don't need to know the details of how a clinician would reach a diagnosis, but you might be curious about how it works. Most of the diagnosis of dissociative disorder is done simply by self-report of symptoms. There is no major personality test that can give a clear differential diagnosis among all of the categories described above.

However, there is one test that I use routinely. In fact, because much of my practice has focused on dissociative disorders, I give this test to every one of my new patients. It's called the Dissociative Experiences Scale, or DES (Bernstein & Putnam, 1986).[1] An online version of the test is available at http://www.traumadissociation.com/des.

The DES consists of 28 questions. Each question asks what percentage of time, from zero to 100%, a particular kind of symptom is experienced. Some of the questions reflect the common kinds of dissociation that most people experience at one time or another, such as "Some people find that sometimes they are listening to someone talk and they suddenly realize that they did not hear part or all of what was said." Other questions describe symptoms that are less common, such as "Some people have the experience of finding themselves dressed in clothes that they don't remember putting on."

Many psychological tests have complicated scoring systems and need to be scored and interpreted by a trained professional. The scoring of the DES, however, is quite straightforward and can easily be done by a lay person. You add up the responses to all 28 questions and divide the total by 28. The resulting score is a number between zero and 100.

The interpretation of the score is not as straightforward, so it's important not to jump to diagnosing a patient (or yourself) based on this score alone. Table 1 below shows the average score and the approximate range for each of the groups studied by the researchers.[2] In fact, the ranges

---

1 **For therapists:** There's also a slightly more recent version called the DES-II (Carlson & Putnam, 1993), but the items are the same as the original. The 1993 article contains a printable version of the test, with permission for it to be copied for research or clinical purposes.

2 The average scores are from the Carlson & Putnam [1993] article; the ranges were listed in the original article by Bernstein & Putnam (1986).

found by the researchers were even larger than the numbers shown here; for each category, I've listed the range where the bulk of the scores fall. As you can see from the table, there's a great deal of overlap in the ranges of scores among the various diagnostic categories. A person with a score of 10, for example, could belong to any of five groups. You can't say with certainty that a person with a given score fits into one and only one category.

Table 1: Median Scores and Ranges on the DES for Various Diagnostic Categories

Category	Median Score	Approx. Range
Normal Adult	5.4	2 – 12
Agoraphobic	7.41	2 – 32
Anxiety Disorders	7.0	
Affective Disorders	9.35	
Eating Disorders	15.8	
Late Adolescence	16.6	5 - 25
Schizophrenia	15.4	2 – 32
Borderline Personality Disorder	19.2	
PTSD	31	8 – 40
DDNOS	36	
DID	48	30 - 80

For this reason, the authors of the DES consider it a research instrument rather than a diagnostic test. It would be inappropriate to try to use this one score to pin down a specific diagnosis in most cases. In practical terms, however, the test can be very helpful in telling the therapist — and the patient, for that matter — what the overall level of dissociation is on a day-to-day basis. When I give feedback on the test results, I don't tell patients where their scores fall in the various diagnostic categories, unless they already know that they have PTSD or DID. But I do tell them when the DES indicates that they have a moderate or high level of dissociative talent.

There are also some rules of thumb that can help point the therapist toward certain diagnoses. Normal adults, who may have some trauma in their backgrounds but don't have a dissociative disorder, will usually score between 2 and 12. Normal adolescents tend to score a bit higher, often between 10 and 20. Schizophrenics typically score between 20 and 30, while people with PTSD often fall between 30 and 40. Above 40, it's very likely that the patient has DID or DDNOS.

There's also a special case worth noting, and that's the person who scores 0 or 1. Psychologist Pati Beaudoin (1998) coined the term "metadissociation" to describe this phenomenon: the complete dissociation of any evidence of dissociation. This takes an exceptionally high level of dissociative talent, and clinical experience has shown that such a person almost always has DID.

CHAPTER 5

Dissociative Identity Disorder

Film buffs may remember a classic movie from 1957 entitled "The Three Faces of Eve." It was one of the earliest films to attempt to give a realistic and sympathetic portrayal of what was then known as Multiple Personality Disorder, or MPD. In the film, a very mousy, plain woman named Eve White turns out to have a sexy, outgoing "alter" called Eve Black. These two personality states struggle for control until, toward the end of the film, a new, healthier "personality" emerges, called Jane.

This depiction of MPD was based on the conception that a person could have alternate personalities, called "alters" for short. It was a commonly held view among therapists, particularly psychiatrists, that all of the major alters were essentially equal—that virtually any of them could kill off or merge with other alters and eventually become the dominant personality.

What DID Is Not

In spite of sympathetic portrayals in "Three Faces of Eve" and the later movie "Sybil" — or maybe, unfortunately, because of them — DID is still viewed by most people as something mysterious and rare. Psychiatrists were often taught this view during their training. Even today, many of them will tell you that they wouldn't expect to see more than one or two cases — if that — in a thirty-year career.

The truth is that DID is not rare. This is important for patients and loved ones to know, so they don't feel so alone. The prevalence of DID has often been estimated at about 1-1.5% of the general population (Sar, 2011). That would mean more than 3 million people in North America live with this disorder. Even the most conservative estimates would mean there are hundreds of thousands of cases. And because DID is frequently misdiagnosed, the correct number could be as high as 10 million (Ross, 1997).

This prevalence is also an important fact for therapists. Therapists who have little or no experience in treating dissociative disorders often buy into the misconception of rarity. They may fail to see the signs of dissociative disorder because it doesn't occur to them to look for such signs. Many of the patients who come to me after having seen other practitioners, especially psychiatrists, have been misdiagnosed as schizophrenic, schizoaffective, bipolar, borderline or all of the above.

A similar error therapists often make is they see the signs of dissociative disorder but don't recognize them for what they are. When a DID patient starts therapy and begins to feel comfortable with the new therapist, the system will often begin to drop hints about its existence. If the therapist seems oblivious to those signs, the system will slip quietly back into the background, and the correct diagnosis will be missed. The system is also likely to go back into hiding if the therapist reacts with disapproval, alarm or excitement over a rare "curiosity." (In my experience, the two most common mistakes therapists make with DID are recoiling in fear or becoming fascinated with the intricacy of the system. I'll talk more about the latter in the Epilogue. The Epilogue is addressed to therapists, but I strongly encourage patients to read it as well, so they know what they should be able to expect from a good therapist.)

Another misconception about DID is that it's somehow mysterious and incomprehensible. It's not any more mysterious than the denial used by alcoholics who are not in recovery. One way to think of both PTSD and DID is that they're normal responses to horribly abnormal circumstances. DID begins as the best response the child is capable of making to horrendous trauma. Remember, though, when we use any defense mechanism to an extreme, it becomes a problem in and of itself. The same principle holds true whether the defense is dissociation, denial, isolation, or anything else.

A third misconception about DID is that people who have it are "crazy." Many people still confuse DID with schizophrenia, especially because both conditions may involve hearing "voices." The technical term for what most people call crazy is psychotic, and schizophrenia is, indeed, a form of psychosis, with symptoms that may include hallucinations and delusions. A person with DID may *feel* crazy, especially before she understands what's going on, but she's not psychotic.

Years ago, when I was teaching at a university, I also served as faculty adviser to the Psychology Club. One semester the students decided to sell t-shirts as a fundraiser. The front of the shirts said, "I'm not schizophrenic." The back said, "Me neither."

The distinction between schizophrenia and DID is not trivial. Within the limits of our current knowledge, schizophrenia is incurable. The symptoms can be managed to some degree with medication, but if the medication is stopped, the symptoms return because the underlying illness has not been changed. In contrast, there are no medications that specifically treat DID, but psychotherapy, even without medication, can result in significant alleviation of the dissociative symptoms. As we'll see in the later chapters on treatment, it's even possible to achieve a complete remission of the disorder.

The Change from MPD to DID

In the decades since "The Three Faces of Eve" was first shown, our understanding of this disorder has changed considerably. The name was changed from MPD to DID to reflect that new understanding. What we now know is that no one has multiple personalities. Each of us has only one personality — one core identity — although that personality can become fractionated very early in life. If a child experiences a severe, overwhelming trauma *and* if she has enough dissociative talent, she may split off the memory of the trauma into a dissociated part of herself. If she continues to experience prolonged or repeated trauma, a whole internal system of parts may develop. Some of these parts may simply be fragments, while others may become elaborately detailed and may indeed be experienced by the core as separate identities.

Characteristics of the Core

I encourage my patients to use the terms "core" and "parts" rather than "alter," because I think the latter term reinforces the old idea that different personality states are about equal. They aren't. There is one, and only one, core. She is the original person born with the body, the one who has the birth certificate. She can't die or cease to exist unless the body dies. And she can't abdicate her position to another part.

The core owns the dissociative system, the entire inner world. The good news is that she has the power to control the whole system; when she orders the parts to do something, they can't *not* do it—they must obey her. They even obey all of her subconscious commands. For example, the core may consciously put parts into restraints inside, but then send the subconscious order to let them out again. A more detailed explanation of this phenomenon is given in Chapter 8.

The not-so-good news, at least from the core's point of view, is that she also owns all of the responsibility for the system. One of my patients once (jokingly) asked me if I would stand up for him in court if he robbed a bank or something—after all, I could explain that he was DID and therefore didn't know what he was doing, right? I pointed out that he really wouldn't want me to testify: I would tell the court that the core is ultimately responsible for everything that the system does, whether he's consciously aware of it or not.

As we'll see in the chapter on treatment, it can be extremely beneficial to have the core's cooperation in therapy, so it helps to be able to identify her. One characteristic to look for is that she's the exact chronological age of the body. In fact, she's the only one who is, although other parts may be younger or older than the core. If she hasn't spent much time in the outside world, she may feel and act younger than she is, but she's still aware of her real chronological age. She usually goes by the birth name or nickname. Our observation in the past has also been that the core is the same gender as the body. This does generally seem to be true, although our understanding may shift as we see more research on the possible interplay among DID and gender dysphoria.

Relationships Among the Core and the Parts

There are two major patterns commonly seen in DID, although there are many variations on these two themes. In one pattern, the core is "up front" in the body and is in contact with the outside world. In this case, she's often completely unaware of the inside world, at least on a conscious level. The typical patient I see of this type is a female in her mid- to late thirties, often married with children, and very often in a helping profession. She comes into therapy because she has odd symptoms — hearing voices, finding things in the house she doesn't remember buying, realizing she can't remember anything over a period of hours or even days. It may seem as if these symptoms just started recently.

(That's not actually true—no one who has been severely traumatized is completely symptom-free—but she may have been in denial about more subtle symptoms.) Or she may have been aware of some symptoms for a long time, but they may be increasing in severity to the point that she can't ignore them any longer. In either case, she typically has no idea of what the symptoms mean and may be terrified that she's going crazy.

In the second pattern, the core becomes depleted, often when she's quite young. She feels completely overwhelmed and unable to cope with what's happening to her. In response, she goes inside and creates parts to function for her in the outside world. Sometimes the core remains awake and aware of the outside world, even though she rarely interacts with it directly. More often, though, she creates one or more parts to handle the outside world; then, finding that she feels safer when they're in control, she gives them increasingly greater control and authority. As they become more powerful, they may encourage the core to hide deep inside, even to go to sleep for long periods of time.

The parts can have a variety of different kinds of relationships with each other as well. Remember that in order to be diagnosed with DID, at least one of the personality states—what I'm calling the core and parts— must have amnesia for the thoughts and actions of at least one of the other personality states. But the amnesia doesn't have to be a two-way street. For example, Part A may know everything that Part B thinks and does, but when A goes inside and B comes back out, B may have no memory at all for what happened when A was in control. Or A and B may be completely co-conscious with each other, while the core is amnestic for A and co-conscious with B.

In talking about the relationships within the system, it's also important to note that the parts can't die or be killed off, any more than the core can. Even in the process of integration, the parts don't cease to be; they only cease to be separate.

Switching and Blending

When one part goes completely back inside and another part comes up front, that's called "switching." In old movies, switching may be accompanied by some dramatic sign or gesture — the head dropping onto the chest, the face going blank as if the person is having a *petit mal* seizure. In reality, it's rarely that blatant. There may be a subtle signal — a glance downward, an eye blink just slightly longer than usual — or there may be no outward sign at all.

It's also possible for more than one part to be up front at a time. This phenomenon is called "blending." Blending can have some interesting, and sometimes problematical, consequences. For example, it may look as though Part A is up front and in charge, but then you may find out that Part B is standing "behind" her and controlling her. It can also happen that A and B are up front at the same time and equally aware of what's going on in the moment, but then B unblends, goes back inside *and takes the memory of the experience with her.* A is left standing there, knowing that she's been up front the whole time but with no memory of what just transpired. For example, Bill had a part who was an expert with computers. As long as that part was blended with him, he could make a computer do just about anything he wanted. But when that part didn't show up for work, Bill couldn't even remember how to turn the computer on.

It's this kind of occurrence that can make DID seem weird, confusing, even frightening. It's truly amazing that the human mind is capable of creating these phenomena. But once you know what's happening, these events become understandable — even if decidedly inconvenient at times!

Types of Parts and Their Jobs

Unlike the core, the parts can be either male or female, independent of the core's gender. Each major part may have its own body image, memories, abilities, likes and dislikes, personality style and — sometimes, but not always — its own name. Rather more curious, studies have found that the different parts can have different eye color, different eyeglass prescriptions, different physical symptoms (or the lack of them) — even different CAT scans.

Some parts can age over time, especially with the help of therapy or other healing experiences. But remember that dissociated memories and feelings are preserved relatively unchanged, as if frozen in time. For this reason, parts with untreated memories tend to remain the age that they were when they were created by the core.

The job of every part is to serve and protect the core. That's the only reason for their existence. Within that broad, general mission statement, however, we can identify a number of different kinds of parts based on the specific functions that they perform.

Parts Who Hold Outside Jobs

Some parts hold jobs in the outside world. One part may be the "good mother" to the core's external children. Another may be the part who handles any kind of confrontation. Another may perform some or all of the core's professional responsibilities. Yet another may have had the job of attending school in the first and second grades. The core may have access to all of her own (impersonal) knowledge and skills, or they may be parceled out among many different parts.

This can give rise to a host of interesting issues. For example, if Louisa's 6-year-old part Mary had the job of attending school for the first few years, then Louisa may not be able to do simple arithmetic unless Mary is blended with her. As the core develops more and more extensive co-consciousness with her various parts, she may have the gratifying—and exciting—experience of discovering that she has talents and knowledge she didn't know she had.

The Double

Sometimes the core creates a part that looks and sounds very much like her—so much so, in fact, that it's essentially the core's double. The main difference I've observed is that the double is oftentimes not fully hooked into the core's emotions. When an emotionally charged event occurs, the double may therefore be able to remain calm, even deadpan.

In some cases, the double may function as a kind of CEO, staying up front most of the time and running the show while the core stays safely inside. In other cases, or at other times with the same person, the core or another part may "wear" the double like a mask or a suit of armor.

When it's the core doing it, it means that she's close to up front, but it's as if there's a layer of insulation between her and the double, so that she's shielded from being hurt. When it's another part using the double, it's usually a protector trying to masquerade as the core. The protectors are described in detail in the next chapter.

When a double shows up in my therapy room, it's almost always the latter—a protector trying to convince me that the core is done with therapy and in no further need of my services, thank you very much. (Only the core is allowed to fire me.) But once you know that such a part can exist, it becomes easier over time to spot the mask.

Parts Who Hold Memories

Dissociative systems are created in response to traumatic experiences, as a way to protect the core from experiencing or re-experiencing the intense pain. It makes sense, then, that many of the parts exist in order to hold these dissociated memories.

Some of these parts represent mere fragments with little or no elaboration. They may not have individual names and may hold as little as a few seconds or minutes of memory, or even a few minutes of a single BASK component. It may take many of these fragments to piece together a single memory.

Other memory parts may hold a whole memory. They may even be in charge of a traumatic pattern, so that they hold all of the memories on a specific theme. In this case, the part may actually be a cluster of related parts. If Annie had the job of coming into the body whenever Anne the core was being molested by her older brother, there may be an Annie-at-age-2, Annie-at-age-4, Annie-at-age-5, and so on. They're all recognizable as Annie, but at different ages.

The Sleeping Baby

The "sleeping baby" is a very special part found in some DID systems. After the core, she's usually the most heavily guarded and protected by the system. In fact, many parts of the system may believe that she is the core and will tell you that. (She isn't—remember that the core is the same chronological age as the body.)

If the core experiences early and repeated abuse, she may take the best qualities of herself—the very essence of being human—and embody them in this special part. If there is such a part in the system, she's typically a baby or small child, because she needs to be untouched by the abuse. She holds much or all of the core's creativity, curiosity, joy, and enthusiasm. The core may then put this little part to sleep and hide her as deeply as she can.

If the core is out front, she may be able to retain a connection to this part and her special qualities, at least to the degree that she senses them "in there somewhere." Later in life, if she has been able to achieve a relatively safe and stable life situation, she may spontaneously regain some—even most—of her access to these qualities.

There is one other major type of part: the protectors. They are so important in the person's functioning and in the process of therapy that they deserve their own chapter.

CHAPTER 6

The Protectors and the Critical Voice

Every DID system contains some parts whose job it is to keep the other parts in line. At least some of these parts are typically very harsh and punitive in their methods. They're emotionally abusive to other parts — yelling at them, ridiculing them, shaming them, and so on. They're also physically abusive — on the inside, by hitting or kicking parts or throwing them against walls, and on the outside, by engaging in self-harming behaviors such as beating, cutting and burning. Because of the characteristic way they behave toward other parts — and even toward the core herself — they used to be called persecutors. About 30 years or so ago, however, therapists began to recognize that these parts actually have a positive purpose, in spite of their extremely negative appearance. They started calling them persecutor-protector parts, and then simply protector parts.

Part of my job as a clinician is psychoeducation—that is, teaching my patients about how the mind works in general and how their issues work in particular. Ever since I became a clinician, I've told my singleton (i.e., non-DID) patients about what I call the internal critical voice and my DID patients about the protectors. After some years of this, I realized that I was talking about the same thing in both cases. I now assume that every human being develops this internal protective function. It simply manifests a bit differently depending on the individual. Let's look at the critical voice as it typically develops in singletons, and then we'll see how this same function serves as the protector parts in a DID system.

The Critical Voice

The original, positive purpose of the critical voice is to guide and protect us. At its best, it's what gives us the capacity to be self-directed and to oversee the quality of our own work. Without it, we'd have no way of knowing whether we were doing right or wrong, a good job or a bad job, unless someone else told us. In a rare—and lucky—few people, the critical voice remains a firm but gentle guide, providing just enough guilt feeling when necessary to direct the person's behavior into appropriate channels but letting the guilt go before it despoils her psychological well-being.

For most of us, though, the protective function of the critical voice is vastly overshadowed by the unpleasant way it goes about its job. If you're a singleton, have you ever stopped to pay attention to the chatter that goes on inside your head? There's a self-help book called *Self-Esteem*

(McKay & Fanning, 2000) that I've often recommended to my patients. I like the structured exercises that people can use. One of the very first exercises is to practice listening for the critical voice and to write down everything you hear from it. I encourage you to try it—it may amaze you to find out how much of it is negative and critical, both toward yourself and toward others.

Some of what the critical voice says is blatant. Whenever we say to ourselves, "Oh, that was so stupid!" or "I'm so clumsy" or "I hate my body," that's the critical voice. Oftentimes, though, it learns to be much more subtle than that. As McKay and Fanning pointed out, sometimes the critical voice communicates to us simply with a single word or with a wash of feeling that overwhelms us with a sense of self-blame and inadequacy. It takes practice to relearn how to hear the implied message and put it back into words that we can dispute. Carol was a shy, young woman with significant self-esteem problems. I asked her to read the chapter in the self-esteem book and do the exercise of listening for her critical voice and writing what she heard in a log. When she came in the next week, she had nothing written down. She said, "I don't know. I've been trying and trying, but I just can't hear it. I must be really dumb." I held my breath and simply looked at her. After a few moments, she heard what she had said, raised her head and looked back at me with dawning comprehension. The following week, her log book was full.

The Development of the Critical Voice

Human beings have a negativity bias. What that means is that we're hardwired to pay more attention to negative events than to positive ones. This bias makes sense in evolutionary terms—primitive humans who were better at alerting to danger cues were more likely to survive and therefore to pass their genes on to another generation. In primitive times, the most important cues would have related to physical danger, such as the presence of a lurking predator. In modern times, most of us aren't constantly exposed to physical danger, but it turns out that we also alert to negative sensory, cognitive, and social events, such as sirens, insults, frowns, or the sight of a raised fist.

The critical voice can be seen as a cognitive manifestation of negativity bias. In the normal course of child development, in environments in which the incidence of physical danger is low, the critical voice is very likely a direct result of socialization, the process through which children learn how to be acceptable members of their particular cultures. In Western culture, socialization generally begins in earnest between the first and second birthdays. We don't expect infants to learn manners, and any potential damage they could cause to themselves or their environment is limited by their lack of mobility. Once they begin walking and talking, though, the importance of instilling safe and appropriate behavior is much greater.

My guess is that the critical voice in a singleton is born the first time someone who matters to the toddler says, "No no!" and backs it up with action. Even in normal development, then, the critical voice is born out of trauma. The words "no no" don't initially mean anything to a toddler. They take on meaning when they're accompanied by some kind of negative consequence: a pleasurable activity is stopped; a toy is taken away; the caregiver pulls back, temporarily withdrawing warmth and affection; the child is slapped.

Some of these consequences are merely unpleasant or unsettling, while others are deeply frightening. In either case, the child is motivated to avoid such events in the future. The way they do that is to internalize a schema, a kind of "picture" or concept of the caregiver. (A schema isn't like a photograph. It's more like a diagram of the most important features of something.) If this internal caregiver can learn to say no before the external one does, the child can successfully avoid the negative consequences.

In the case of the merely unwanted consequences — having a toy taken away, for example — once the child is successful at changing her behavior the trauma is essentially processed and resolved, and there are probably no serious lasting effects. The toy is returned, and all's right with the world. Not only that, but in the best possible outcome, when parents are consistent in the consequences they impose, the child also comes away with a positive and empowering sense of mastery: she can choose her behavior, and therefore she has the power to forestall these negative consequences from happening. (Or she can decide that the consequences are worth it this time and do it anyway!)

But consider what happens when the mother withdraws her affection: the implied threat is that the child could be in danger of losing her mother's love forever, and she picks up on it. Even though young children can't articulate their feelings, they're normally quite perceptive and intuitive, and they grasp much more than adults typically give them credit for. In this case, the child doesn't know if she can ever do enough to win back her mother's love. Because she's dependent on her parents for all of her physical and emotional needs, the threat is essentially one of annihilation. That's a terrifying experience and a significant trauma, one that persists long after the original incident is over. The main coping mechanism that the child has is dissociation, so the fear becomes dissociated.

The immediate, short-term effect for the child is very rewarding — on a conscious level, she no longer *feels* the fear. But remember from our earlier discussion that dissociated feelings still have a significant impact. That, I believe, is one reason that the critical voice becomes so powerful and so strongly negative — even in a singleton, it reflects the terror of the consequences of not behaving acceptably.

Characteristics of the Critical Voice

The first major coalescence of the critical voice into a discernible "voice," a discrete and recognizable part of ourselves, seems to occur, on average, at about age 4. Because parts tend to stay the age at which they were created, what this means is that the central essence of the critical voice tends to think like a 4-year-old. Socialization is well established by that time, and the 4-year-old's command of basic language structure is almost as good as an adult's. But a 4-year-old's understanding of the world is very different from that of an adult.

I should add, as an aside, that a second major node of critical-voice thinking seems to develop around early adolescence. This aspect of the critical voice is recognizable by its attitude — oppositional, defiant, sarcastic, and flippant. The resistance contributed by this side of the critical voice has the same defiant quality to it. But even here, the thinking and reasoning stays at a much younger level.

Contradictions

One maddening characteristic of the critical voice is that it can hold completely contradictory thoughts or opinions with no apparent discomfort whatsoever. You cannot win an argument with the critical voice using conventional, adult logic. It will find something to criticize you for no matter what you do. If you decide to give your friend a rather expensive gift for her wedding, your critical voice will say that you're stupidly extravagant; but if you let it talk you into buying something less expensive, it will call you stingy and selfish. The only healthy way to deal with it is to refuse to argue on its terms.

When the critical voice holds contradictory opinions or beliefs, it can flip rapidly back and forth between them, but it doesn't actually ever hold them at the same moment. It was one of my patients who taught me the enormous healing power of the AND. When you hold two seemingly contradictory statements at the same time and link them with "and" instead of "but," you are acknowledging that neither one of them negates the other. "My mother did the best she could to be a good parent AND she was intensely and constantly critical." That gives you the larger truth instead of only one facet of it.

Absolute Thinking and Overgeneralization

The critical voice can't hold the AND because, like any 4-year-old, its thinking is entirely too black-and-white. Something is good or bad, right or wrong. It doesn't understand exceptions or extenuating circumstances. It operates by inflexible rules and demands that you obey them. Anytime you hear yourself using the word "should" or any variation on it—must, ought, have to, need to, supposed to, etc.—it's likely that you're speaking from your critical voice. We do sometimes say, "I should go to the store today," meaning "it would be a good idea," without any critical tone. But with a little practice, it becomes increasingly easy to pick up on the difference.

The always-never dimension of its thinking also causes vast overgeneralization. Instead of calmly acknowledging to ourselves that we were five minutes overdue for a meeting this week, we find ourselves exclaiming, "I'm always late!" Even worse, the overgeneralization about our behavior slides into global, negative beliefs about ourselves: "I'm a failure."

Another corollary of its absolute thinking is that the critical voice has no tolerance for ambiguity or uncertainty. Waiting for an answer is agonizing, so it will often impulsively slam the door on a promising new relationship or new endeavor before we have a chance to find out whether it might actually work out.

Wrong-Headed Protection

The critical voice believes that if it calls you a name first, it won't hurt as badly when someone else does it to you. This hypothesis actually works to some extent with physical pain, and I wonder if that's where the critical voice gets the idea. If you bite your lip after you've stubbed your toe, the pain impulses from your lip compete with the pain impulses from your toe and partially obscure them. That's why rubbing the toe works, too—the sensation of rubbing interrupts the pain messages being sent to your brain.

Unfortunately, the same approach does *not* work with psychological pain—quite the contrary. When I allow my critical voice to call me stupid, I create that schema inside. Then when someone else calls me stupid, the hurtful message gets in because it has something to match to. If I weren't holding that schema, the message would simply bounce off. I might feel surprised by it, I might even laugh at it, I might feel sad that this person apparently has a low opinion of me, but I wouldn't feel hurt.

Try this exercise: Think of something about yourself that you like and that you're completely confident about. It can be anything—perhaps you have a good singing voice, you're tall, you're a good cook, you're a good debater. Now imagine how you'd feel if someone tried to contradict you. If you're really completely confident about this quality, nothing the other person says can faze you.

For John, it was being smart. He knew he was smart, without a doubt. His critical voice sometimes tried to make him feel bad for not doing enough ("If you're so smart, why aren't you president?"), but it couldn't shake his certainty. He was even a card-carrying member of Mensa, the high-IQ society. So if someone tried to tell him he was stupid, he did *not* think, "Gosh! What's wrong with me?" Instead, his internal response was, "I wonder what's the matter with *that* guy?!"

Understanding this particular characteristic of the critical voice also helps us to understand a basic principle of modern popular psychology. You've probably heard the assertion many, many times that no one else can make you angry. It's true. The fact is that no one can *make* you feel — or do or say or be — anything if you're not so inclined. Of course, someone who knows you well knows where your "buttons" are. He can choose to do something knowing that there's a high probability that you'll wind up feeling angry or hurt — or happy, for that matter. But he can't actually make you feel any of those feelings. What makes you feel angry or hurt is your own critical voice. It hears the negative message, takes it in, matches it to a schema you already hold, and beats you up with it. To be even more precise, the other person's critical voice speaks to yours, and the better the person knows you, the more accurately his critical voice will be able to target your internal schemas. But *all* of the actual damage comes from your critical voice, your own personal "Trojan horse." (If you remember Greek mythology, the Trojan horse represents something that defeats you from inside your own walls, rather than from outside.) On the positive side, though, the corollary is that if you were able to clear out all of those old schemas and the traumas that created them, you wouldn't have any buttons left to be pushed, and no one's critical voice would be able to find a target.

Unfortunately, virtually all of us have chinks in our armor somewhere. In my experience, the more unresolved trauma we have (including everyday trauma), the more vulnerable we are to the machinations of the critical voice, and the more power it has to distort our thinking. Another of its techniques is to apply strong filters to our experience — like mud-colored glasses instead of rose-colored ones. It readily absorbs negative information while screening out positive input. There's a rule of thumb in popular psychology that it takes ten positive comments to outweigh one negative one. For people who have an especially powerful critical voice, the ratio may be much higher, to the point that they simply don't hear positive input at all—or if they do, they find a way to negate it. Unlike John in the example above, they have no certainty about their good qualities, only doubts and fears.

Egocentrism

As I mentioned earlier, psychologist Jean Piaget described stages of cognitive development in children. The stage of concrete operations doesn't begin until about age 7. Before that, from roughly age 2 to age 7, children are in what he called the preoperational stage—and since the essence of the protector system is stuck at 4 years old, it's more or less permanently at this stage. One characteristic of preoperational thinking is egocentrism. When we're talking about cognition, "egocentric" is not the same thing as "egotistical" or "selfish." It refers to the fact that a young child sees himself as the center of the universe and simply isn't capable of stepping out of that position to take another person's point of view. He's truly not aware that there *is* another point of view: "Ooo, my toe hurts—can't you feel it?"

If you have a young child, there's an easy way to demonstrate this characteristic. Get a piece of paper that has a different color or picture on each side. Show both sides of the paper to the child and make sure that they can accurately name both pictures or colors. Then hold up the paper between you so that each of you sees only one side. Ask the child which one *you* see. A typical 4-year-old will name the picture or color that *they* see. They literally can't shift their point of view to understand that someone else's would be different.

An emotional consequence of this cognitive characteristic is that children tend to see themselves as responsible for everything that happens. If mommy and daddy get divorced, the child believes it's because they were being bad and their parents were fighting over them.

This way of thinking dovetails well with the critical voice's primary role of protector. It's a terrible experience to feel helpless, and our critical voice tries to protect us from such feelings. From its point of view, it's often much better to see ourselves as responsible for an event than to admit we have no control over it. Unfortunately, the natural conclusion of this line of thought is that everything is our fault. (Of course, not being bothered by contradictions, the critical voice is also capable of causing us to feel helpless and incompetent in other situations.)

One serious consequence of egocentrism is that most of us tend to take things personally far too often. We interpret things as being about us when they aren't. An important example of this thinking is what I call the victim question: "Why did they do that *to me*?" A somewhat better question is, "Why did they do that?" The answer might be that the person is re-enacting a trauma that was done to them, or that they're a sadist who has gone over to the dark side — we may never know. But the point is that the perpetrator's behavior tells us only about them — it tells us nothing about the person on the receiving end.

Another cognitive consequence of egocentrism is that the critical voice believes in mindreading, in both directions. Being unable to entertain a different point of view, your critical voice believes that it knows what another person is thinking: the person holds exactly the same thoughts that it does—all negative, of course. If you have doubts about yourself, then the other person must also think you're incompetent. Think about how many times you've started a sentence with some version of, "I know you'll think I'm crazy...." It also believes that the other person knows what you're thinking. It's probably this quality that leads to the rather peculiar belief, quite prevalent in our culture, that if you care about me, you'll know what I want for my birthday without my having to tell you. (Since you *can* read my mind, if you *don't* it must be because you don't care.) If you stop and think about it, this belief is clearly irrational, but that doesn't make it any less powerful.

An Unusual View of Time

Another characteristic of the critical voice is that it doesn't have a concept of linear time. In linear time, time flows in only one direction. One moment happens after another after another. Yesterday is gone forever, and tomorrow hasn't happened yet. But to the critical voice, time is nonlinear. All moments exist equally in the present moment—past, present and future are all one. It's this characteristic that allows the critical voice to rewrite history so easily. If you know something today, your critical voice believes that you should have known it yesterday—because yesterday and today are all the same thing. If you buy a stock and it tanks, your critical voice will beat you up because you should have known that the stock was going to go down.

This characteristic causes many people to constantly second guess themselves, to revisit their decisions over and over, because the penalty for being wrong is very painful. The critical voice causes us to blame ourselves for things that were not our fault and events that could not have been foreseen.

I've come to believe that this view of time is also the main cause of trauma replication, when a person puts himself into situations that repeat the same kind of trauma over and over. An example would be a woman who had an alcoholic father and marries one alcoholic husband after another. On one level, the critical voice is trying to rewrite the story with a better ending this time around. But I think there's a deeper level as well: the critical voice believes that it can rewrite history. If the woman can reform her husband and make him into a "better man," it will also change the past and rewrite her experiences with her father.

Primitive Moral Reasoning

When a 4-year-old thinks about right and wrong, her moral reasoning isn't based on internalized, high moral principles such as a belief in the sanctity of all life. Her judgment rests on a much more primitive basis: the external consequences of a behavior. A behavior is bad if she gets punished for it; a behavior is good if it gets her something she wants. Of those two, however, avoiding punishment is by far the stronger motivation for toddlers and young preschool children.

If you stop and think about it, it's obvious why this would be true for children who are being abused. Avoiding punishment may be literally a matter of life and death. However, it has also been observed to be true in many children who are not severely abused. My guess is that, in our culture, the typical nonabusive parent generally doesn't require very young children to "earn" basic necessities or small treats through good behavior. Thus the cause-and-effect connection between behavior and consequence is much clearer for negative behaviors and consequences than for positive ones. As a result, the main orientation of the critical voice is punishment, and in order to avoid external punishment, it becomes very punitive itself. It's capable of punishing us with deep feelings of hurt, shame, guilt, embarrassment and even — in at least some cases — physical symptoms.

In more extreme cases, the critical voice causes us to contemplate suicide. In its way of thinking, there may be many kinds of events that are, indeed, worse than death. This is especially true because the typical 4-year-old doesn't understand that death is permanent and irreversible. Cases of pediatric attempted suicide are rare, fortunately, but when such children are interviewed, they almost invariably say something like, "I was gonna shoot myself so when I saw them at school on Monday they'd be real sorry for teasing me." Thus your critical voice can easily believe that it's protecting you by urging you to die.

Hope Phobia and Catastrophizing

The critical voice is also hope-phobic. It doesn't want us to hope because disappointment is so excruciatingly painful. Remember that the critical voice isn't the least troubled by inconsistency. Its reason for existence is to protect us from pain, but it's perfectly capable of inflicting pain internally in order to protect us from pain coming from outside. It doesn't realize that human beings die if they have no hope. Consequently, it's very good at catastrophizing, at predicting the worst possible outcome. More than that, it will tell you that it's only being realistic and any other way of seeing things is pie-in-the-sky foolishness.

This quality can have a significant impact on the course of therapy. Having no hope, the critical voice doesn't want change. It doesn't believe that positive change is possible. It doesn't want to try anything new, and it doesn't believe that the therapist's methods can possibly work. From its viewpoint, it's unproductive, unsafe, and just plain stupid to go ripping open painful memories when nothing can be done about them anyway. Thus, it resists. I've come to believe that everything we call "resistance" in psychotherapy, and in life in general, comes from the critical voice. Years ago, resistance was something of a dirty word in psychotherapy, something for the therapist to push through or break down. Seeing it in this light, however, helps to remind us of the positive intention underlying resistance. As wrong-headed as the critical voice's methods may be, its essential purpose is to protect.

While we're on the subject, I'd also like to suggest to you that almost every negative thought and feeling you have comes from the critical voice. One major exception to this is the sadness and grief we feel in response to loss—that's a natural response that comes from the heart. There also appear to be some fears that arise from natural causes. But as you begin working on identifying the old traumas and the feelings and beliefs that grew out of them, a good place to start is to assume that every time you feel hurt, fearful, angry, guilty, ashamed, or judgmental, your critical voice is right in the middle of it.

Rule Making

Another part of the critical voice's function is to make rules to govern our thoughts and behavior. The more powerful our critical voice is, the more stringently and punitively the rules are enforced. For example, one very common rule is "Don't ask questions." If we dig a little more deeply, we're likely to find the belief that asking questions makes you look stupid or weak, which leads to painful humiliation. The purpose of the rule, therefore, is to protect you from being humiliated. Once established, rules like this can show up in countless variations and can affect almost every facet of our everyday lives. For example, one patient insisted on having her daughter's hair cut short even though the daughter wanted to let it grow out. When we explored why the mother was so adamant, it turned out that long hair requires a special kind of brush (another rule), she didn't know where to buy one, and her critical voice absolutely forbade her to ask. Even without our being aware of it, the critical voice often controls much of what we feel, believe, and do. The next time you find yourself doing—or not doing—something without knowing why, ask yourself what rule your critical voice is enforcing.

Irrational Thinking

Notice from these examples that critical voice beliefs and rules are almost always irrational. That doesn't make them any less powerful—quite the contrary. When I was in graduate school studying child development, I learned a very important principle: there is no such thing as maladaptive behavior in children (Jones, 1974). Another way of saying the same thing is that every behavior—and belief — we acquire serves a positive purpose. It meets a need of some kind. The behavior or belief only becomes maladaptive when we transfer it to a different situation where it doesn't work. In adulthood when these rules no longer apply, they become inconvenient at best and severely maladaptive at worst.

Magical thinking falls into this category. The human mind seems to be hardwired to see patterns in objects and events, even when they don't actually exist. This kind of thinking also causes people to attribute much more power to thoughts and wishes than they actually have. As a result, children — and even adults — sometimes have trouble distinguishing between thoughts and feelings on the one hand and actual behaviors on the other. If a young child gets angry at her father and yells that she wishes something bad would happen, and then the father has an accident, the child genuinely believes that her wish caused harm to her father. The reverse is also true: the critical voice believes that if we don't think about something, then it isn't real, it didn't happen.

Magical thinking is a natural feature of a 4-year-old's cognition but, like all of the other critical voice features, it can wreak havoc when we allow it to color our judgment as adults. It causes us to draw conclusions about cause and effect that are completely erroneous. I apologize if I'm stepping on toes here but, in my opinion, the belief that "everything happens for a reason" is an example of this kind of thinking. It can sometimes be comforting in the moment, but when something painful happens, there are really only two interpretations, one bad and the other worse. The bad one is that the painful event happened in order to teach the person a lesson. They must have needed to learn something. The worse interpretation is that they're being punished. In either case, people often spend a lot of time and energy trying to figure out the lesson or the reason for the punishment. If they keep looking, they may indeed find something to blame themselves for, even if it had no real connection with the painful event. Abuse survivors may blame themselves for everything they suffered. Not finding an external explanation can cause even more prolonged and agonized searching.

The fact is that some events are simply random. We aren't the center of the universe, and we're not responsible for everything that happens, no matter what the critical voice wants us to believe. In contrast to this irrational thinking, I offer a different view to my patients: if I spend six months planning a garden party and it rains that day, it didn't ruin everyone else's plans just to teach me some kind of lesson. I'm not that important.

As an aside, I will add this thought: even though we didn't cause the painful event to happen, the old cliché about lemonade from lemons applies. We can always ask ourselves what we can learn and how we can grow from the experience.

Characteristics of the Protectors

The protector parts in a DID system are simply another manifestation of the critical voice, and they have the same kinds of characteristics. In order to understand the protectors and why they function as they do, it's important to keep in mind that, at their hub, their understanding of the world is that of a 4-year-old. They're hope-phobic, punitive, rigid, and often inconsistent; they have a nonlinear sense of time; they make and enforce an elaborate system of rules; they draw erroneous conclusions about blame; and they don't believe that positive change is possible, so they don't like meddling psychotherapists.

Above all, their job is to protect the core from further pain and abuse. Note, however, that they don't have the same concern about the other parts. In fact, they'll gladly sacrifice the welfare of the other parts in order to protect the core.

A part who holds a trauma memory is trapped in that moment of time, much like the figure in the famous painting by Edvard Munch called "The Scream." The protectors care little or nothing for the pain these parts are experiencing. Their only concern is to keep those parts locked in their dissociative prison so that the pain can't reach the core.

Contradictory Beliefs and Behaviors

Like the critical voice, however, the protectors have no difficulty maintaining entirely contradictory beliefs and behaviors. Although they'll fight to the death to protect the core from being hurt from outside, they're perfectly capable of hurting her themselves if they think it's necessary to protect her. They may even re-create the actions of the abuser, so that the core behaves as if the trauma were happening now. One patient, for example, was severely abused as a child. She was also dependent on her abuser for all of her basic needs, and he would sometimes withhold food as a way of controlling her. In consequence, her protectors evolved a complex set of unbreakable rules around food and eating. As an adult, she was unable to go into a grocery store to obtain food for herself. She couldn't buy a refrigerator because she wasn't allowed to think ahead about eating, storing food, or preparing meals. At times, her protectors forbade her to eat at all, in order to "toughen her up" in case the abuse and deprivation happened again. The protectors' rules became so pervasive that they completely paralyzed many areas of daily functioning.

Nonlinear View of Time

It may seem absurd that the protectors would be acting as if the abuse could happen at any time, as many as 30 or 40 years after the event. But remember that the protectors don't have a linear view of time. For the protectors, as well as for the parts still stuck in the memory, then is now. Nor does it matter to them that the abuser is dead; they don't understand that death is permanent. And they're easily powerful enough to blend with the core and swamp her thinking. She then believes that these are her own thoughts and feelings, especially if she doesn't yet know about blending and unblending. She obeys the rules compulsively and rarely, if ever, thinks to question them. Oftentimes, she has no understanding of why she has these rules; she only senses that, if she breaks any of them, something terrible will happen.

Large and Scary Appearance

Just as the critical voice typically coalesces for the first time at about age 4, so does the first cluster of protectors. When a DID patient enters therapy, it's not unusual for the first protector that's encountered to look like a very large, shadowy figure in a dark cloak. If the core gathers her courage and pulls the cloak open, however, she finds that it's a scared little 4-year-old trying very hard to look big and threatening.

Hierarchy

The protectors are usually arranged in a hierarchy, with the older, more powerful ones concealing themselves in layers behind the smaller ones. The older protectors generally range in age up to 14 or 15, sometimes (though rarely) to 16 or 17. I've never met a protector who admitted to being a grown-up — presumably because if they were grown up, they would have to behave by adult rules. The littlest protectors are easy to reach, and they often melt with no more than a kind, caring voice. The further up the hierarchy you go, however, the more difficult the protectors are to deal with.

An Unchanging View of the Core

Parts who have experience with the outside world, including protectors, aren't frozen in time the way that memory parts are. Even though they tend to stay the same age as when they were created, they can grow and learn. However, the protectors' view of the core does essentially stay frozen. The core creates the inside system as a young child because she believes that she can't survive knowing and feeling all of her traumas. The protectors continue to see her that way — as a child who will be destroyed if she tries to take on the crushing burden of her memories. And because they genuinely believe that, they do their best to make sure that the core continues to believe it as well.

Imagine a young queen—someone similar to Queen Victoria of England, perhaps—who comes to the throne before she's legally of age. She would have one or more regents appointed to help her rule. But the regents, being powerful men themselves, might well believe that they could do a much better job of running the country than a silly little girl. They might convince her to give them more and more power, so that she could be free to play and enjoy herself. They couldn't insult her to her face, but they might send her subtle messages that she really wasn't capable of handling matters of state. If this process started early enough, she would believe them—and she might continue to believe them even after she reached the age of majority. She would be the queen in name, but they would rule the country in fact.

The protectors often hold this kind of world view. The core has given them a great deal of power, and they feel that they know much better than she does how the system should be run. The fact that the core, as an adult, has all kinds of emotional, intellectual, social, and financial resources that she didn't have before doesn't make any difference to them. Their way works, they say—never mind the devastating and potentially deadly symptoms that the core is experiencing—and no other way of doing things can be trusted as safe.

Because the protectors genuinely see the outside world as dangerous, they keep sending strong, subconscious messages to that effect to the core. The less safe the core feels, the more power she cedes to the protectors. When a patient is having significant difficulties getting the critical voice/protectors under control, it's a good bet that she has a long-standing traumatic pattern around a perceived lack of safety. As one patient put it, "From birth on, I never felt safe anywhere."

One aspect of the healing, then, is for the core to take back her power from the protectors. That is, literally, an empowering experience and, ultimately, a deeply satisfying one. In the beginning, though, it can be very frightening. That's why it's helpful to begin therapy with techniques that give the core alternative strategies for controlling the traumatic material and for standing up to the protectors.

Before we move on to talking about treatment, however, it's vital to remember that the protectors are not evil. I frequently remind the patient's whole system that the protectors have done an immensely valuable job and that the patient wouldn't be alive without them. When I can, I let them know that I care about them just as much as I care about all of the other parts. We don't want them to stop doing their job; we just want to change how they do it. It's not their existence that's the problem, it's their behavior.

For example, sometimes a protector part will take on the appearance of an abusive parent, so that it seems to the core as if the parent is actually inside of her. The reason for doing this is that it makes the system better at predicting the parent's behavior and therefore at avoiding at least some of the abuse. The core and other parts often hate this protector. They may even want to kill him. What I point out, however, is that this part has taken on one of the most difficult jobs in the whole system. He's like a sewer worker, doing an extremely dirty and unpleasant job so that the rest of the system can live more comfortably. Even though we may temporarily exile him, or put him into containment until we can teach him how to do his job in a different way, he deserves our respect and appreciation, not our hatred or contempt.

CHAPTER 7

A Model for Treatment

The most widely accepted approach to the treatment of trauma is a three-phase model. It's considered the standard of care — meaning that any psychologist or psychotherapist who treats trauma should be familiar with this approach and skilled in its use. There are many variations on this basic theme, some suggesting four phases rather than three, but the model I like the best is the classic one described by Brown, Scheflin and Hammond (1998). It's based on an amazingly comprehensive review and distillation of over a century of research and clinical experience, and it's held up well even many years later. The three phases described by Brown et al. are containment and stabilization, memory processing, and self and relational development.

As a point of information, four-phase models differ from this view in that they include evaluation as the first phase. Whether you consider the initial evaluation as part of the containment phase or as a phase in itself, it is indeed an essential part of the process. A good intake will assess the patient's presenting problems and symptoms, especially whether she's experiencing any suicidal ideation. The therapist will also need to know an outline of the patient's history, insofar as she can remember, including such areas as family relationships, school experiences, friendships and dating and, of course, any accidents, illnesses and significant traumas.

One thing I *don't* do as part of the evaluation—or the continuing therapy—is to try to create a "map" of the DID system. This used to be a common approach in treating DID: the therapist would create a diagram of all of the different parts as they emerged, with their names, their ages, and their interrelationships with other parts. Some therapists even pushed patients to name parts who didn't have names and to work at describing them as fully as possible. I haven't found that helpful. On the contrary, in my experience that kind of exercise is in exactly the wrong direction: it actually tends to solidify the dissociation, because it makes the parts more distinct and separate than they were naturally.

Containment and Stabilization

The overall goal for the first phase of treatment is to give the patient tools to help contain the traumatic material and to stabilize his life, both inwardly and outwardly. The major themes of this phase are mastery and empowerment.

This phase is tremendously important. In many ways, it's the most important phase of therapy. Whether you're the patient or the therapist, you won't want to skip this part of the work or gloss over it. The containment aspect of this phase refers specifically to the containment of traumatic memories and the feelings and behaviors that arise from them. Even if you aren't able to accomplish anything else—and with managed care companies approving as few as 10 sessions per year, there may not be time for much of anything else—the patient's quality of life will be considerably higher if she has these tools to work with. The frequency and intensity of flashbacks and other post-traumatic symptoms will be significantly reduced, and she'll actually get to have a life while she's doing the therapy. The processing of the trauma memories will be faster and safer if the traumatic material is first contained, because then it becomes possible to work on it one piece at a time, with much less danger of flooding. You don't want to do trauma processing in crisis if you can help it, whether it's a crisis related to past trauma or a current crisis such as a job loss, because there's a far greater risk the patient will simply be retraumatized rather than helped.

Perhaps even more important than these positive results is that successful containment provides the patient with a sense of mastery over the trauma. She's no longer at the mercy of the winds, being buffeted or bowled over without warning. Instead, she feels empowered, and she develops confidence that she can be in control of her own life.

Having a stable life situation also aids the process of therapy. For that reason, work in this phase might include doing whatever can be done to strengthen the patient's primary relationships, broaden her psychosocial support network of family and friends, even improve her decision-making or people skills in order to increase her job security. It might also entail working with the patient, in conjunction with her other practitioners, on issues related to her physical health. For example, the therapist might refer the patient for a medication evaluation or help her develop a record-keeping system to keep track of her blood sugar. All of these elements help to provide solid ground for the patient to stand on while accomplishing the next phase.

Memory Processing

In the second phase of treatment, the goal is to process the traumatic memories in such a way that they're converted to normal, narrative—i.e., nontraumatic—memories. One way to conceptualize this shift, as I mentioned in Chapter 3, is that the BASK components (behavior, affect, sensation, and knowledge) become un-dissociated and reintegrated in the person's conscious awareness of the present moment. The critical aspect that allows the shift to happen is the person's awareness of complete *safety* in the present moment. When a part of the mind is stuck in a trauma, it doesn't know that the person survived and went on to be okay. It's afraid to find out the end of the story because it truly doesn't know how it came out. When all of the BASK components are reassembled in the context of good therapeutic technique, the memory becomes unstuck *and* that part of the mind learns that the core—the whole person—survived.

Another way to think about how this shift happens comes from our increasing understanding of the physiology of trauma. Simply put, a traumatic experience creates specific neural pathways in the brain, connecting certain cues or triggers with physiological reactions. When one or more of these cues are encountered, they trigger electrical and chemical changes in the brain, which in turn trigger the physical and emotional reactions we recognize as the symptoms of PTSD. On the other hand, when we process a memory in therapy, we're causing a new neural pathway to be created by re-pairing the cues with a sense of calmness and safety. This is the mechanism underlying the technique called systematic desensitization. From clinical experience, it does appear that the memory needs to be "activated" — i.e., present in conscious awareness — at least to some extent, in order for the rewiring of the brain to occur. We now know, however, that it's not necessary for the person to re-experience every gory detail of the trauma at full intensity in order for the trauma to be re-paired — and repaired.

On an experiential level, what the patient feels when a trauma is truly cleared is that it no longer has an emotional charge. She can remember that the event happened, but it doesn't have the power to hurt or frighten her. It no longer controls how she thinks, how she feels, or how she behaves in the present moment. She doesn't have to keep managing the thoughts and feelings or find a way to live with the experience. It really is *done.*

Self and Relational Development

In place of its formal title, I often refer to the third phase as "clean-up." This phase deals with the kinds of issues that, because of the trauma, the person never had a chance to work out in the course of normal development. It also includes the kinds of typical, garden-variety problems that we frequently see in patients who have experienced a "normal" amount of trauma in their lives, but not so much that they became DID.

As the name of the phase implies, many of these problems revolve around issues of identity and self-esteem. A patient may literally not know who she is, apart from her erstwhile identity as a trauma survivor. She may need to explore her most basic likes and dislikes. Even her sexual identity may be called into question, especially if she has a history of childhood sexual trauma. One very common task for survivors is to come to feel oneself, genuinely and thoroughly, as a healthy, vibrant whole, and not as "damaged goods." There may also be issues of irrational guilt—for having survived, for example, or for not having been able to stop the abuse, or for not having protected younger siblings.

Other issues have to do with learning how to have healthy relationships with other people. Some patients may need to learn basic social skills. For example, they may not have any idea of how to chitchat, which can make it difficult to form new friendships, at least outside of the survivor community. Others may need practice in being assertive, both with other people and with their own critical voice/protectors. One of my patients was astounded to learn that she had the power to make choices about how she responded to other people—and that she could, in fact, make very good choices for herself. Another vital skill that almost all trauma survivors need to learn is how to set and enforce good, healthy boundaries.

Of course, the phases are not quite as neat as I've described them here. It's not that you'll completely finish with the first phase before going on to the second and then the third. They intermingle. You might well find, for example, that a relationship issue won't wait on hold for a year or two—or more—until you can get to phase three. And you'll probably have to do at least some trauma processing before you have all of the phase one elements in place. Some DID patients cycle through the phases more than once: after the core has worked with the material from one cluster of parts through the first two phases and into the third, another cluster may appear with new material, causing her to loop back to phase one. But the overall model provides excellent guidelines to help both therapist and patient maximize the safety and the effectiveness of the therapy.

A variety of powerful tools has been developed that can significantly help therapist and patient address the goals of the various phases. The next three chapters describe in detail some of the conventional tools that I've found to be the most useful and creative in the treatment of trauma.

CHAPTER 8

Containment Tools to Enhance the First Phase of Treatment

A s you learned in the previous chapter, the major themes of the first phase of treatment are mastery and empowerment. When the core is successful at containing a traumatic memory for the first time, she begins to realize that she can be in control of her own life instead of being constantly at the mercy of unpredictable flashbacks. As more and more of the traumatic material is contained, she also begins to realize that she no longer needs to allow her critical voice/protectors to control her either, with their rigid rules and constant punishment. Like the young queen with her regents, she finds that she can rule the realm herself, and with a much less repressive regime.

In order for the core to take control back from the protectors, she needs new tools — new ways of doing things. The new tools we can give her are much more effective than the protectors' old ways. In addition, these new tools reduce dissociative symptoms, instead of creating them as the protectors' methods do. In this chapter, we'll focus on some powerful tools to help with containment and stabilization.

Contracts, Directives and the Importance of Language

Early on in my practice, I made fairly frequent use of contracts. A contract is an actual, written document, signed by the patient, agreeing to do or not do a specific behavior or class of behaviors. The most common contracts are to prevent self-harm and suicidal behavior, but they can be written for anything as needed.

Therapists don't always like to admit this, but there are obvious limitations to contracting. If a patient decided to die by suicide, she could simply go ahead without calling me as agreed, and there would be nothing I could do about it. At its best, a contract works because the patient's word means something to me, and I mean something to my patient. If the patient can't stop cutting herself for her own sake, she may be able to do it because it's important to me as her therapist. That can't be the final answer, of course—ultimately, she has to do it for herself—but it's fine as a temporary bridge until we get to that point. If she's unable to hold hope for herself, because her thinking is still swamped by her critical voice/protectors, I'll ask permission to hold it for her until she can find her own again.

With DID patients, contracting can be a little more complicated, because many of the parts consider themselves autonomous. However, there are some specific phrases that can help to make the contract much more effective. One statement that appears at the bottom of every contract I write is, "I understand the essence of this contract. There are no loopholes." It's virtually impossible to write a contract that fully describes an almost infinite range of variation on a given behavior. In addition, many DID patients are extremely bright, and they often have at least one "jailhouse lawyer" protector part, a legalistic, argumentative type who can split hairs with incredible finesse. This statement stops a lot of the wrangling over what the contract did or didn't say.

Another sentence that appears on all of my contracts with DID patients is, "Whoever signs below signs for all." With this statement in place, parts can't argue that they weren't party to the contract and therefore aren't bound by its terms.

I still use contracts sometimes, but more often nowadays I ask patients to use directives. A directive is simply a statement—an order, if you will—that the core sends inside to the inner system. The content of a directive can be almost anything, from simple to deadly serious. For example, the core might direct that all of the child parts are to stay inside while the core is at work, so that they don't come up front and reveal themselves in an embarrassing way. Or the core might order a protector part to go into "time out" to keep her from offending other people, stealing things from stores, or killing the body.

This is one of the reasons why it's helpful to have the core up front, or at least present, in therapy. Remember that the core's body, mind, system—all of it—belong to her.

They *are* her. She has the ultimate power to decide what she chooses to think or do. (This applies to singletons as well.) So no matter how much they argue, the parts cannot disobey a direct order from the core. For that reason, an excellent phrase for the therapist to keep in mind is, "Now I know the core can hear me…." Even if the core was deep inside and asleep just a moment before, she will now be able to hear everything that's said on the outside.

The biggest potential problem with directives is that the inner system will obey subconscious directives from the core just as readily — even more readily, sometimes — as conscious ones. It's easy to see why that might be the case. If the conscious directive to the protectors is *"Please be quiet and sit down"* while the subconscious directive is "COME AND SAVE ME!" it's understandable which one they would react to first. I've come to believe that some of the most powerful words in the English language are "I can't stand it!" That phrase, or any variation of it — I can't handle this, I can't do it, this is too much, etc. — is heard as a directive to "Help me! Do something!" and it instantly galvanizes the entire protector network into action. If they still have the power to do so, the protectors may yank the core inside, so that she loses awareness of hours or even days. If they can't implement a complete switch, they may blend with her and swamp her thinking.

In either case, the part who takes control has the job of alleviating the pain, fear and anxiety by whatever means it can. Because some of these protectors are among the youngest, their coping mechanisms may have a childlike directness to them. It's not unusual for these coping mechanisms to take the form of substance or behavioral addictions, for example.

Lee had a part we referred to as the Shopper. When Lee felt wounded by a harsh criticism or put-down, the Shopper would take over and go to the mall. But it turned out that it wasn't only spending money or having something new and pretty that made Lee feel better. The Shopper tended to go to the more expensive stores, and it was the personal attention from the store associates that was the most important element. It made Lee feel special, and that was what she craved after a childhood of emotional abuse and deprivation.

Not all of the protectors are childlike, however. As I discussed earlier, some of them are angry teenagers. Barbara had a teenage protector named Patty. Patty held a great deal of Barbara's anger, and when she was out front, she often wound up offending people and driving them away. Barbara repeatedly put Patty into some form of restraint to try to keep her from coming up front, but somehow Patty kept getting loose and wreaking havoc. It turned out that when Barbara felt threatened, her fear became the subconscious order, "Patty, come save me!" The restraints around Patty would vanish, and Patty would rush forward to deal with the perceived threat.

I strongly encourage my patients to listen to themselves, to take responsibility for their inner language, and to excise the word "can't" from their vocabularies. True, there are some genuine "can'ts," mostly grounded in physical reality. I can't jump 10 feet off the floor. I can't see clearly without my glasses. For almost everything else, I ask them to substitute "I haven't been able to do it yet." Rather than "I can't stand it," it's much less likely to trigger the protectors to say, "This is painful and difficult for me." It's also entirely okay to add, "And I don't like it!"

There's another verbalization that can also help significantly. When the core sends a directive to the inside system, she can add the following instruction: "You are to follow this directive regardless of whether you hear, or think you hear, me say something to the contrary." If the core is currently in therapy, she might add, "This directive is to remain in effect unless my therapist and I jointly decide it's time to change it." This phrasing helps to prevent subconscious directives from overriding the core's conscious intention.

There's another subtle but significant difference between "I can't" and "I haven't been able to do it yet" that's worth noting. The latter is a simple statement about a present condition. The former has an element of prediction about the future—it implies "and I won't ever be able to." As the core is working on paying more attention to her inner language, it will help if she also listens for statements that reflect this predictive element and remembers to convert them to simple, factual statements about the present.

Notice that there's a theme here: we all have control over what goes on inside our heads. The messages from the protectors (or, for a singleton, the critical voice) are beliefs, not facts. They may contain some small kernel of truth ("I was five minutes late to a meeting this week" vs. "I'm always late"), but for the most part they have very little grounding in present-day reality. The core can choose to dispute the distorted aspects of the messages and replace them with a more accurate understanding.

Another change the core can make in her inner dialogue is to stop arguing with the protectors. Have you ever tried arguing with a 4-year-old? You will never hear young children say, "Ah yes, I see your point. You've convinced me." The child keeps coming up with buts and questions and just doesn't stop until you declare an end (or give in). Even worse, as soon as you allow yourself to be sucked into an argument, you've already lost ground, because you've tacitly admitted that whatever you're talking about is open for debate. The same goes for the protectors. It's not possible to win an argument with them. Whichever side the core takes, they will take the other. The healthy way out of this situation is for the core to remember that she is the adult and refuse to argue.

It's also possible to take this one step further, beyond choosing not to argue. As challenging as it may seem sometimes, the core doesn't have to have an adversarial relationship with the protectors. Remember that no matter how offensive and wrong-headed they sound, they're trying to protect. They always have a positive purpose for what they're doing. (It's essential for the therapist to remember this as well.) If the core can identify what problem they're trying to solve, she may be able to find a healthier alternative. Instead of yelling back at them, she can then take an entirely different tack by saying, sincerely, "Thank you. I know you're trying to help. And I've got this."

The Quintessential Safe Place

One of my favorite tools for containment is a beautiful guided imagery exercise called the Safe Place, which was developed by sociologist Jim McCarthy (1995). McCarthy had interviewed and consulted with dozens of therapists and hundreds of clients across the country, and many of them also contributed to the Safe Place design.

The concept of a "safe place" isn't new. Many patients invent one spontaneously, and a number of psychologists have suggested variations on the basic theme. I used to simply encourage patients to develop whatever form of safe place they liked. However, this particular model has several unique features, and each part of it is designed to give the safe place very special therapeutic benefits. For that reason, I've renamed this imagery the Quintessential Safe Place to distinguish it from generic safe places. I ask the patient's permission — and I recommend to you — to install the Quintessential Safe Place exactly as described, at least initially. I also let people know that the core has the power to reject the visualization and tear down the Quintessential Safe Place if she decides after the installation that she doesn't like it. So far, no one has.

It's very important to have the core present when the Quintessential Safe Place is installed. Like everything else in the inside system, the Safe Place is created by the core, belongs to her, and exists to serve her needs. I prefer to have her up front, if possible, so that she and I can communicate directly. But it will also work if the core is listening from inside. Even if other parts "assist" in the construction of the Safe Place, the critical factor is that the core ratify it — put her stamp of approval on it, so to speak. Remember that the protectors cannot disobey a direct order from the core. By the same token, they cannot trash the Safe Place if the core has ordered that it stand.

Remember, though, that the Safe Place, and all the tools that go with it, are not only for patients with DID. We've all been traumatized in one way or another, and we all have parts and aspects, even if they're not as clearly defined as in a DID system. This approach works just as well with singletons as it does with DID.

The Quintessential Safe Place visualization described below is written in the language of a hypnotic exercise, and a therapist suitably trained in hypnosis may prefer that approach. But it isn't really necessary to do a formal hypnotic induction—most people with any kind of dissociative talent slip in and out of trance quite naturally anyway in the course of daily life. You can simply allow the patient (or yourself) to sit back and relax, with closed eyes if that's comfortable, as the visualization is presented. Because of the level of detail, you may wish to install only one or two components of the Quintessential Safe Place at a time, pausing in between to allow time to assimilate the image fully.

Would you like to have a recording of the Quintessential Safe Place in the author's own voice? It's available at www.karjala.com/courses for a nominal charge.

Imagine that you are in a mountain meadow, a beautiful meadow filled with grass and wildflowers and butterflies. It's a sunny day, and the sky is a perfect shade of blue, with fleecy white clouds. It's a large meadow, about 300 to 500 acres, completely surrounded by tall peaks, so that it's completely enclosed and safe. One very important aspect of this very special place is that it's always the present day here, never the past, so whenever you go into the Safe

Place, you are in the present, not in a moment in the past.

Over the entire Safe Place, I'd like to suggest that you put a dome of golden light. If you like, you can think of this as divine light. You can also extend the dome underneath the ground, so that it makes a complete sphere of protection. The dome of light acts as a shield over and around the Safe Place, so that no one can enter it without your permission.

[Check to make sure that the meadow and the dome are in place before proceeding.]

More or less in the middle of the meadow, I'd like to suggest that you build a house so that the core, and any parts the core invites in, have a comfortable place to stay in when they're in the Safe Place. It's a one-story house, with no attic or basement. It's built on a foundation of granite or bedrock at least 10 or 12 feet thick. There is no back door, and the windows cannot be opened from the outside. When you're in your house in the Safe Place, you are completely safe, and no one and nothing can come at you unexpectedly.

[Pause to check progress.]

Inside, there are as many rooms as you need — living room, bedrooms, bathrooms, a dining room that always had fresh, healthy food, and so on. You can come back and fill in the details later, but for now, just know that the house has everything that you could want or need.

[Pause to check progress.]

A short distance from the house, perhaps 20 or 30 yards away, if you look around you might find that there's a rocky outcropping with a little waterfall flowing down it into a beautiful little pool. If you look closely, you'll find that the water has sparkles in it of the same golden light that makes up the dome. This is your healing pool. Parts of you can come to the pool, bathe in the water, drink the fresh water from the waterfall, and be healed inside and out.

[Pause to check progress.]

About the same distance from the house, but in a different direction, you might want to put in a bank vault. You've probably seen a bank vault in the movies or on TV or even in real life. It has very thick, strong walls and floor and ceiling, all made of metal. If you open the door and walk inside, what you'll find is that it has whatever kind of storage system is perfect for you. It may have shelves or drawers or bins or lockboxes, whatever kind of storage works best for you. The vault will hold as much as you need it to hold – it never gets full. What you can do is to take painful thoughts and feelings and memories that you're not quite ready to work on yet and store them in the vault. This will keep these thoughts and feelings and memories safely contained, because the vault will hold anything that you need it to hold. By using the vault, you'll also know exactly where these thoughts and feelings and memories are stored when it becomes time to work on them. And what do we often do with our most precious objects? We put them in safety deposit boxes in bank vaults. Even these painful memories are very precious, and they're stored in a safe place until you're ready to deal with them.

For the moment, though, I'd like you to come back out of the vault, close the door and turn the big handle that's sort of like the steering wheel on a car. Now, if you walk around to one side of the vault, I'd like to suggest that you put in a slot like the night deposit at a bank. A night deposit has baffles inside so that things can be put in, but they can't get back out. This way, if other thoughts or feelings or memories come up at a later time, you can simply slip them in through the slot, and you don't even have to open the door of the vault. Things will go directly into storage until you're ready to take them out.

[Pause to check progress.]

Another feature I'd like to suggest for your Safe Place is a small cottage. This can serve as your Time Out Cottage. Remember that protector parts are not usually allowed in the Safe Place. One very important rule of the Safe Place is that no one is allowed to hurt anyone else. In order to be invited in, parts must be able to promise that they won't hurt anyone else, physically or emotionally, and most protector parts who are still actively being protectors can't do that. They're excluded from the Safe Place and can't get through the dome of light. So you might want to put a bubble of golden light on the outside of the dome with a cottage inside it. It's a very pretty cottage with many of the same features as the main house – very comfortable furniture and pillows and so on. It has big picture windows, so that it's always bright and cheerful inside and filled with healing energy. When you have parts who are acting out and need external

control over their behavior to keep them (and others)
safe, you can put them in the cottage. It's a place where
you can have protectors go so that they're not in the
main Safe Place but they are in a protected Time Out.

Notice that the particular design of this Safe Place provides layers of containment. The core has a special, private study inside the house, inside the Safe Place. Trauma memories are kept in storage containers inside the vault, inside the Safe Place. Acting-out protectors are kept inside their own Time Out Cottage, inside a bubble of golden light—but outside of the Safe Place, so that they can't accidentally escape there and cause havoc.

Virtually all patients—and even some therapists— seriously underestimate the importance of adequate, effective containment. One therapist called to consult with me because her patient was strongly resisting bringing up an area of traumatic memory. As we talked, it became clear that the only containment the two of them had worked out for this memory was a cardboard box with a ribbon around it tied in a bow. I pointed out that boxes leak, cardboard disintegrates, bows become untied. A better approach is to think of traumatic material as equivalent to radioactive waste and needing the same level of safety precautions. When the therapist had the patient install the Quintessential Safe Place and put the memories in the vault, the processing was able to proceed much more smoothly.

Once the central aspects of the Safe Place have been installed, there are many other details that can be added. The following are some examples of elaborations to the main house and the Time Out Cottages:

- a living room, with comfortable couches and chairs and pillows, where the core and parts/aspects can come to meet and talk.

- a dining room, with a table that always has delicious and healthy things to eat and drink, so that no one in the Safe Place ever goes hungry or thirsty.

- enough bedrooms and bathrooms for all of the parts. Some of the bedrooms will be for just one part, others may be dormitory style, and some may be nurseries for the littlest ones.

- a playroom or recreation room in the house, and you can have in this room all of the kinds of toys and games and activities that the core or any of the parts would like to have, all of them safe.

- a private study that's just for the core. This is a place where the core can go to rest or think or write, and no other part of the system is allowed to enter unless the core invites them. So even within the Safe Place, within the house, the core has a special place to go that no one else can go in without the core's permission.

- outside the house, right next to it, a playground, with slides and swings and perhaps a tree fort— anything that the core and parts might enjoy.

- in the Time Out Cottage, a special kind of guard or shield that comes down over the doorknob and prevents it from being opened from the inside. The shield is designed to detect the level of emotional intensity in the cottage. When a part in time out has calmed down and is no longer out of control, the shield retracts, and the part is able to open the door and come out of the cottage.

Individuals may also find that they want to make modifications to the Quintessential Safe Place to suit their own particular needs. In some cases, for example, the core has a whole separate house of her own, not just a study in the main house. If a patient already has a safe place, I often suggest that she lift it into the new Safe Place. One patient created a whole amusement park in the back of her Safe Place. Some of my patients have healing pools that are deep enough to swim in, but others may want one only a few inches deep. One patient with a fear of drowning didn't want to have water in her pool at all; instead, it she designed it with many-colored swirls of sparkling energy. Another patient had parts who were triggered by drinking water. They drank magic sparkling cider instead.

On rare occasions, a patient may find the image of a mountain meadow unacceptable as a safe place. In such a case, it's permissible to find another, more suitable image. Two that have worked in the past are an island far out in the ocean and a Southwestern mesa with very tall, steep sides. The point of these types of settings is that nothing can sneak up on the Safe Place without being seen. Even when the setting is changed, however, all of the other elements and the basic rules of the Safe Place should remain the same.

The main thing to listen for when any change is proposed is that the change is being made in a positive, healthy direction—it is not being made by the protectors to sabotage the Safe Place by incorporating trauma triggers. If the core hasn't ratified the construction of the Safe Place, or if she subconsciously allows it, protectors can sneak in. It's important, therefore, to talk about the reasons for wanting the change. For example, the reason that the house has no attic or basement, or even a second floor, is that those areas are often associated with abuse. Even color may be highly significant. One patient remembered being abused in a room with green walls, so there was no green anywhere in the house in her Safe Place.

With the main elements installed, the patient may want to draw or diagram the Safe Place. She may also want to give a copy of the drawing to her therapist. This will help the therapist visualize it as the patient sees it and help both of them keep track of any changes that are made over time.

With the Safe Place in place, the core can begin to invite parts to come in. (With a singleton, I might simply ask her to visualize herself as she was at different ages, sometimes with the help of photographs, and invite those younger "selves" into the Safe Place.) A part who has been invited into the Safe Place can leave and re-enter at will. Occasionally, a child part who has been in the Safe Place will wander out and appear up front when it's not appropriate for her to be there — e.g., when the core is at work or is engaged in physical intimacy. If that happens, the core doesn't have to do anything special to fix the situation; she can simply remind the part to go back into the Safe Place and play or go to sleep, and the part will almost always know how to do that. She can also ask an internal helper to come and pick her up.

Some patients find a way for a part to be in the Safe Place and up front at the same time. But not everyone can do that, so when a part is needed up front to go to work, for example, she has to leave the Safe Place temporarily and return at the end of the day. In general, it's a good idea for parts to stay in the Safe Place when they're not needed elsewhere.

Once invited, parts who hold impersonal knowledge or skills or who perform jobs in the outside world can come straight into the Safe Place without any special preparation. On the other hand, remember that protectors are not allowed into the Safe Place at all unless they promise not to hurt any other part. In other words, they can continue to help protect the system, but they must significantly change how they go about doing that. It's important that the core send a directive inside stating this rule.

The parts who hold trauma memories need more than a simple invitation to enter the Safe Place. It's tremendously important to begin getting them into the Safe Place as soon as possible, but it has to be done in such a way that their traumas are contained. It would undermine the central purpose to have these parts running around loose, even in the Safe Place, with all of their memories and feelings still susceptible to being triggered at any moment. In the next chapter, you'll learn about tools that will help the core unblend from memory parts, get them safely into the Safe Place, contain their traumas, and more.

CHAPTER 9

Advanced Tools for Use with the Quintessential Safe Place

In the previous chapter, we talked about the major details of the Quintessential Safe Place: the main house, the healing pool, the vault, and the time-out cottages. These elements form the basis for a very effective system of containment. They provide not only for the containment of traumatic material, but also for the restraint of parts who are acting out and potentially putting the whole system in danger.

Once you have the central elements of the Safe Place installed, however, you can construct and add many more details. The possible elaborations are limited only by the patient's and therapist's imaginations.

In addition, there's a wonderful set of tools that has already been developed to enhance the Safe Place. These tools can be used to make the Quintessential Safe Place even more useful and powerful. As I mentioned at the end of the last chapter, these tools are designed, among other things, to help the patient get memory parts into the Safe Place in such a way that the traumatic material is contained and the core is not retraumatized. There is a tool that can help the patient find all of the parts involved in a particular memory, so that they can all be brought into the Safe Place at the same time. There is even a tool that will help the core unblend from other parts when necessary.

The Globe of Light

Perhaps the most important of these tools is the globe of golden light. When a flashback comes up, the therapist can have the core surround the whole trauma scene with a globe made of the same golden light as the dome. The core then lifts the globe up and into the Safe Place. If the core goes near the trauma scene, she may be sucked into it, so she'll need a designated helper who is not the core for the next step. The helper reaches into the globe of light and gently guides any and all parts out of the globe—and therefore out of the trauma scene—into the Safe Place. Remember that the Safe Place is always the present day, so as the parts step out of the globe, they're automatically brought into the present. When all of the parts are out of the memory, the core visualizes squashing the globe of light down to softball size. The reason for this is to make sure that all parts are out of the globe. No parts are ever put into the vault—only the globe containing the memory. If it won't squash down, there's still at least one part inside. If you can get it down to softball size, it's too small for anyone to be left inside. Then the globe is put through the slot on the side of the vault.

Once the memory is put away, the helper takes the now-liberated parts to the healing pool, where they bathe in the healing water. They also drink fresh water from the waterfall, so that any residual hurts are healed inside and out. The helper makes sure they have fresh, new clothes, and they can have anything they want, from a bathing suit to a ball gown. Afterwards, the parts can run and play, or go into the house to eat or rest—whatever they would most like to do.

This technique is the central application of the Safe Place. The more memory parts the core puts in the Safe Place and the more trauma memories she contains in the vault, the fewer flashbacks she'll have. Even before she comes anywhere close to processing the memories, this one change can provide significant stabilization in her inner and outer life. In addition, finding that she *can* control her inner life, that she no longer has to be at the mercy of unpredictable emotional storms, can be a profoundly healing experience.

An important side note: When the Quintessential Safe Place was first being developed, it was thought that the memory parts could stay there, safe and happy, *until it was time to process the memory*. Then the core would need to call them up so that they could participate in the healing process.

But that never seemed right. On the one hand, I was telling the parts that they were forever safe in the Safe Place. On the other hand, I was instructing the core to have the parts come back up and re-experience the traumatic memory. Even though it was in the service of healing, I felt I was lying to them.

Since then, however, I've come to an important realization: it's not the parts who need to do the healing, it's the core. In fact, the memory cannot be fully resolved until the core first re-owns it as hers, as an element of her own true history. Asking the parts to do the processing is moving in exactly the wrong direction. Whether you're single or multiple, it simply isn't possible to process a memory that isn't owned as yours.

Nor are the parts needed, if you stop and think about it. Using the globe of light, all of the elements of the memory are put into the vault — the parts no longer hold them. The vault allows the core to select one memory — or even one memory element — at a time to work on, so that she doesn't become overwhelmed and flooded.

Thus the memory parts are, indeed, forever safe in the Safe Place. The core may choose to visit them from time to time and take comfort in seeing them there. Alternatively, and without particularly thinking about it, she may simply allow them to fade away, since they're no longer needed.

Returning to the globe of light, a critical aspect of this technique is the identity of the helper. It cannot be the core or any part who has anything to do with the particular memory, because if they reach into the memory, they'll get sucked right into the flashback. I used to suggest that the core ask for a part to come forward who had no connection to the memory. Over time, however, I came to find the concept of angels very useful, and whether they're viewed as literal or metaphorical makes no difference. A few of my patients have told me that they're uncomfortable with angels, and we've come up with a workable substitute — one decided to use "grandmother spirits," for example — but many people seem to like having angels in the Safe Place. And they make wonderful helpers. They're completely immune to flashbacks, because they weren't affected by any of the trauma memories. They're infinitely kind and patient and will rock and sing to child parts for as long as needed, even days at a time. They don't even need sleep.

Curiously, several of my patients, completely independently of each other, noted an interesting observation about their angel helpers. What they found was that angels will do any positive thing the core asks them to do, but they won't take initiative. The steps don't have to be spelled out every time; the core can simply say, "Please take care of the parts in this memory," and the angels will follow through with the whole procedure. But the core has to ask. One aspect of empowerment is taking personal responsibility for one's own work, and this observation seems to be an elegant reflection of that principle.

The Light Net

The same golden light that's used for the dome and the globe can also be formed into a light net. If a flashback has come up, the core may want to use the net to make sure that all of the parts involved in the memory are taken into the Safe Place at the same time. Or the core, even while not in flashback, may become aware of a painful memory that she wants to put into the vault. She sweeps the light net through the entire inside to find and pick up the desired parts with their memories. The net will pass through any other parts or objects. Once all of the parts have been gently picked up by the net, the net becomes a globe of light, and the core can follow the procedure described above to get the parts into the Safe Place.

The Silver Screen

Another useful tool is the silver screen, designed by psychotherapist Karishma Brough (1995). It's about the size and shape of a regular screen door, but where the mesh would be are very fine lines of silver, and everywhere the lines cross, they sparkle.

The original purpose of the silver screen was to screen out "psychic crud," particularly the crud that we're carrying for other people. For this purpose, you visualize yourself holding the screen in front of you, and you step forward into the screen while pulling it through you at the same time. As Brough taught it, you also keep in mind the person whose crud you're carrying and, as you step through the screen, you say, "I keep what is mine for my life's work, and I lovingly send back to you what is yours for your life's work." Notice that the statement is made without anger or resentment. The underlying concept is that each of us has to do our own life's work. No one else can do our work for us, and we can't do anyone else's, even if we were willing. An even more thorough cleaning is accomplished by pulling the screen front to back, from side to side, and from above the head to below the feet.

Another purpose of the silver screen, perhaps more applicable in the current context, is unblending. The core can use it to unblend from parts, and parts can use it to unblend from each other. For example, if a part comes up in flashback and overwhelms the core, the core can pull the screen through herself, front to back, to unblend the part back out. As soon as the core is unblended, she should also immediately put a globe of light around the part so that the part can't reblend. Then the part, along with the flashback trauma scene, can be lifted into the Safe Place as before.

The unblending will be accomplished more easily if the therapist also suggests that the core speak calmly and gently to the part. The message for the core to convey is that she's not pushing the part away or trying to bury him again. It's not that the core doesn't like him or doesn't want to hear from him. On the contrary, the best help the core can give the part is to put him in the Safe Place, and the therapist and the core will both be able to hear him much more clearly when he's no longer stuck in the memory. Usually, parts can hear the reassurance in that message and respond accordingly.

Golden Rain

Protectors are not allowed in the Safe Place, for obvious reasons. The Safe Place would not be safe for anyone else if the protectors could enter freely. An easy way to set this up is to suggest the core make a rule that no one is allowed to enter the Safe Place unless they promise, with complete truth, never to hurt another part, physically or emotionally. Protectors can't make that promise. But every once in a while, for a variety of reasons, the core may subconsciously allow them to sneak in. When this happens, the protectors may do quite a lot of damage to the Safe Place.

At its essence, what makes the Safe Place safe is not that it can never be harmed. What makes it safe is that the core has total power over what happens there—which means that any damage can be easily fixed. If protectors sneak in and trash it, the core can take the golden healing water and make it rain everywhere in the Safe Place, even inside the house. That will restore everything to its proper condition. The golden rain evaporates as soon as it's done its job, so there's no worry about soggy sofa cushions.

Sometimes the protectors can fool the core into thinking that the Safe Place has been trashed even when they haven't been able to get inside. Remember that the protectors believe that these new-fangled tools won't work and will only cause pain and disappointment, so they'll often do anything they can think of to stop the core from using them. The protectors create this false image by putting an overlay, like a plastic film, over the outside of the golden dome. The effect is like looking into a house through a very dirty window—everything inside looks dirty and dingy. The answer, of course, is to use the golden rain on the outside surface of the dome to wash off the overlay. The core will then be able to see that everything in the Safe Place is just as it should be.

Another use for the golden rain is if parts are blended and the silver screen isn't getting them unstuck; raining on them may work instead. Indeed, if anything goes wrong in the Safe Place, the therapist can suggest that the core rain on it. It can't hurt, and it may solve the problem.

The Magic Wand

Another very useful tool, the magic wand is a truth-compelling device. It can be used by the core or any part she designates. Whenever a part or object inside is suspected to be something other than it appears to be, the core can touch it with the wand and say, "Show me your true form now." The true nature of the part or thing will be revealed. Whatever is touched by the wand has to show you or tell you the truth about itself, and that includes protectors.

For example, one of my DID patients has an angel for each part in the Safe Place. A child part came out in a session and reported to me that her angel "wasn't acting like an angel," but instead was being quite mean to her. I described the wand to her, told her how to use it, and suggested she see what happened. It turned out that the supposed angel was, in fact, a protector. The core had the protector escorted out of the Safe Place. When the part looked around, she found her angel in a painting on the wall. As soon as she saw her angel, the angel was able to step out of the frame and come to her side again.

The Containment Box

Sometimes we're anxious or angry about something in the present day, and there's nothing constructive that can be done about it at the moment, but we just can't seem to let it go. A classic example is when you've had a medical test, and the results won't be back for a week. There is absolutely no positive purpose served by stewing about it — whatever the results are going to be, you can't change them after the fact. This kind of problem is often a contributing factor in insomnia; even when we're successful at pushing away the anxiety during the day, the thoughts may come flooding in as soon as our head hits the pillow.

The vault in the Quintessential Safe Place is not generally the best tool to use for present-day, ongoing feelings. It's designed more for long-term storage, to contain traumatic material for months or years until the patient is ready to process it. In fact, one side benefit from installing and using the Safe Place is that patients develop greater affect tolerance — that is, they gradually become *more* able to sit with their present-day feelings and experience them in real time, instead of numbing or dissociating them. This change occurs because, with the traumatic material contained, they can allow themselves to feel their feelings without being triggered into flashback.

For the most part, it's healthier to acknowledge our feelings and allow ourselves to feel them than to stuff them. However, it's not healthy to simply sit and stew, which is what tends to happen when there's no positive, constructive action we can take to fix the problem. Fortunately, there's a tool that can help in this situation. Imagine a beautiful box about the size and shape of a silverware chest. It can be made of whatever material is just right for you — titanium or silver or marble or teak — so that it's completely sturdy and safe. It was originally called an angel box because many patients choose to visualize it as carved all around the outside with angels; angels are powerful and can hold anything. But you can enhance your box with anything you like that will make a powerful container. The inside of the box is lined with the most perfect fabric. Again, it can be anything you like — silk or cotton or wool — in the most perfect color or pattern for you. If you look more closely, you'll also find that the entire lining of the box is made up of pockets.

When you're feeling anxious or upset about something, and the anxiety isn't serving any useful purpose — for example, in motivating you to action — you can take whatever it is and put it in the containment box. Use the silver screen in all three directions to release yourself from every aspect of the anxiety-provoking thoughts, put everything into a pocket of the box, and close the lid. You can repeat this procedure as often as necessary to keep putting all of the thoughts away until the time is right to do something constructive about the issue.

The same technique can also be used for anger — not because there's anything bad or wrong with being angry, but because we don't tend to make our best decisions when we're caught up in strong emotion. By putting the anger and all of its aspects into the box, you'll be able to think more clearly about possible solutions and what's truly best for you, instead of exploding and quite likely making the situation worse.

CHAPTER 10

Tools for Memory Processing

One way to do memory processing, when the patient is ready, is to add another feature to the Safe Place: an annex to the vault that functions as a healing room. This technique provides layers of containment around the traumatic memory so that it can be processed more safely, reducing the likelihood that the patient will become retraumatized during the time that she's dealing with the memory. The underlying principle on which the technique works is a form of systematic desensitization.

Like the Safe Place itself, this technique was initially developed as a hypnotic exercise. I presented the original version of it at a conference of the American Society for Clinical Hypnosis in 1999. However, the patient and therapist can decide together whether or not to use a formal induction while creating this visualization.

Here is the description of the Healing Room:

Right next to the vault, I'd like to suggest that you build another building. The main room of this building is very like the vault itself — it has thick, strong walls and floor and roof, so that any memory you put inside will be safely and completely contained, just as it has been in the vault. In this room, however, the inside walls are bare, because you won't be using the room for storage.

In addition to the main room, the building also has a small entranceway. You could think of it as a foyer, an antechamber, or an airlock. It's built of the same construction as the main room and is just as sturdy. On one wall of the entranceway, next to the door leading to the main room, there's a dial with numbers from 0 to 10. This dial will control the intensity of the memory, and you'll be able to set it to whatever level you're ready to experience.

If you look at the side of the building nearest the vault, you'll notice that there's a connection between the two buildings. It might be a cable, or it might be a tube, like the pneumatic tube you used to see at a bank drive-through. This connection will allow you to move one memory at a time, or even one piece of a memory, from the vault into the Healing Room.

After describing the whole process to the patient in detail, so that she knows exactly what to expect — including the fact that she can stop it at any time — the first step in using this tool is to decide what memory to work on. The patient describes the memory to the therapist in as much detail as she can remember without getting into the feelings. The object is to talk about the memory, not to re-experience it.

The next step is to divide the trauma into manageable sections. Sometimes, if the event is relatively small, it may be possible to process the whole memory at once, but more often it helps to take it in segments. When I first started using this approach for dealing with single-incident traumas, such as car accidents, I would divide the memory into at least three time periods: the events leading up to the trauma (e.g., driving on the highway), the central trauma (the crash itself), and the aftermath (being pried out of the car, being treated in the emergency room, etc.). However, I usually found that the central trauma needed to be further subdivided. For one patient, for example, the first part of the central trauma occurred when she looked up at her rearview mirror, saw the other car hurtling toward her, and knew that she was powerless to do anything before it struck her vehicle. We worked on processing that segment separately from the moment of the crash.

Since the original conception of this technique, I also realized that a chronological approach was not the only way in which to divide up the memory. It may be helpful to process individual BASK (behavior, affect, sensation, knowledge) components separately — the feeling of powerlessness knowing that the accident is about to happen, the physical sensation of one's chest hitting the steering wheel — even if they occurred at the same time.

Once the therapist and patient have the workable segments of the trauma defined, they can then decide on the order for processing them. I don't recommend working on them in chronological order, but rather in order of intensity, from low to high. If there are only the three time segments, it would be the lead-up, the aftermath, and then the central trauma.

With the segment chosen, the next decision is the intensity level, from 0 to 10, that the patient will experience during the round of processing. At 0, the patient experiences no emotions or physical sensations; she's simply a detached observer, as if she were watching a movie. At 10, she experiences the full impact of the original event or component. Most patients start the first round at 1 or 2, and if they're having trouble picking a number, I'll usually ask whether 2 seems about right.

The final step before the processing involves transferring the memory from the vault into the Healing Room. The core, in the Safe Place, can simply ask the vault to transfer the memory. Alternatively, if the core prefers, she can ask an angel or other helper to go into the vault and send the memory over to the Healing Room.

As we discussed earlier, the goal here is to convert the traumatic memories to normal, narrative—i.e., nontraumatic—memories. The critical aspect allowing this change to happen is the person's awareness of complete *safety* in the present moment. The therapist's calm voice during this technique serves as an anchor to the present day and the safety of the therapist's office.

When the patient is ready to do the actual processing, I give the following instruction for the first round of processing:

> *Go into the entranceway of the healing room, close the outside door, and look at the dial by the inside door. Set the intensity to ___, as we agreed. When I say "go," I'd like you to open the inside door and go into the Healing Room. I'm going to count ten seconds aloud, and you'll be able to hear me clearly. When I say "stop," I want you to come out of the Healing Room and shut the door. Are you ready?* [Patient says "yes" or gives affirmative signal.] *Very good. And...GO. One, two, three* [counting at about one number per second]*, four, five, six, seven, eight, nine, ten. STOP. Come out of the Healing Room and close the door. Take a big breath. Very good!*

I ask the patient to tell me what the experience was like and how she's feeling at that intensity level. The plan is to repeat the process as many times as needed until she reports feeling comfortable with that level. On subsequent rounds, therefore, she may choose to keep the intensity the same or to change it. If the current level is reasonably comfortable, the patient is probably ready to increase it on the next round.

Ideally, it should *never* be necessary to decrease the intensity. If that happens, it's up to the therapist to make sure that the patient isn't being overconfident or—worse—sabotaging and retraumatizing herself by taking on too much at once.

It's my experience that patients rarely need to increase the intensity only one point at a time. A typical pattern would be to master the experience at a low level (around 2), then jump up to 4 or 5, and then to around 8. And that may be enough. It was once thought that a trauma had to be re-experienced in all of its intensity in order to be healed. But clinicians have discovered over the last three or four decades that's not the case. It's often just as effective—and less painful—to have the patient send a directive inside to her subconscious to allow her to experience the trauma "just enough" to clear it. With that directive in place, a level of 7 or 8 may be "just enough."

A different way the Healing Room can be used takes advantage of its special features, especially the ability to call up just one BASK component at a time. This technique may be helpful, for example, when the core has consciously recalled only fragments of a memory. In this approach, the core furnishes the Healing Room with a large easy chair. On the wall opposite the door, there's a big screen TV with a remote control. Rather than using a time limit, the core makes herself comfortable in the chair. When she's ready, she calls up *only* the cognitive component of the memory—no emotions or body sensations. If she's working from fragments, she may start with a fuzzy image on the screen and then allow it to become clearer and clearer, like a photographic image emerging in a tray of developing fluid. One caution about this technique: it's very important not to dig for the memory or to start filling in gaps with suppositions about what "must" have happened. Digging and guessing will only muddy the waters and make it harder for the core to sort out what really did happen from what she imagined—which may ultimately make it harder to resolve the trauma.

The Healing Room technique has several layers of containment built into it to make the processing safer. The Healing Room is located in the Safe Place, where the core has the power to control what happens as well as helpers to assist her. There's an anteroom or airlock between the Healing Room and the rest of the Safe Place so that memories can't accidentally leak out. The memories aren't processed in the vault itself, where the potential might exist for several memories to flood in at once. Instead, the material can be processed one memory, or even one component, at a time. This feature also allows the core to recall memories safely, because she can allow the cognitive component to emerge without being overwhelmed by the emotions. The intensity dial allows the patient to titrate the affect—that is, to gradually increase the level of emotion, and even physical sensation, that she's able to handle. The ordering of the segments performs the same function, by allowing the patient to start with low-intensity components and build up to more intense ones. Finally, the therapist's audible counting puts a time limit on the experience, so the patient knows that the experience has a definite end. This feature also specifically counteracts the time dilation effect that often occurs in sudden trauma, when it seems as if the event is going on and on, even when it's only a few seconds in real time.

As the patient processes more and more of the memories in the vault, her skill, confidence, and sense of mastery will all increase. This may allow her to process larger chunks or even whole memories at a time.

Even more important, as more and more of the traumas are processed, the symptoms—the negative thoughts, feelings, and behaviors—caused by them will begin to disappear. At some point, the focus of the therapy shifts from alleviating the problematic symptoms to strengthening the patient's positive, adaptive skills. At this point, the therapy moves into the third phase, of self and relational development, discussed in the next chapter.

CHAPTER 11

Finishing the Therapy

As I mentioned before, the final phase of therapy focuses on self and relational development. Trauma not only causes the development of negative feelings, beliefs and behaviors, it also prevents the development of positive ones. Processing the memories removes many of the negatives, but it doesn't automatically replace them with healthy alternatives.

The objectives of the various phases were discussed in Chapter 7. In the first phase, the focus is on getting the traumatic material into containment, so that the patient's functioning can be stabilized, both internally and in the outside world. This work helps to provide the stable platform for the patient to stand on while doing the work of the second phase, which is the actual processing of the traumatic memories.

As the traumas are processed and the symptoms arising from them are alleviated, the therapy shifts into its final phase. The main work for the patient in the third phase includes such tasks as establishing a healthy sense of identity and self-esteem, developing emotional independence, and setting good boundaries. Some of the questions to be explored about identity, such as sexual orientation, may have major implications for the patient's entire lifestyle, and those questions may give rise to a whole secondary set of issues, especially if they affect other people around the patient. Other questions may be surprisingly basic, such as finding out what the patient's favorite color is and what foods she likes or doesn't like.

The effects of trauma are far-reaching, and survivors may not know even simple things about themselves until these effects are cleared away. For example, Susan's mother always made tuna noodle casserole for Friday supper. The meal almost always started in stony silence and ended with a screaming fight, because her mother was furious that her father stopped at a bar and got drunk on the way home. For much of her adult life, Susan got sick to her stomach every time she so much as smelled canned tuna. It was only after the trauma was identified and treated that she was able to try tuna casserole and tuna salad and decide for herself whether she liked them.

The work of the third phase also includes learning how to have healthy relationships. This may mean polishing basic social skills. For example, the patient may have become proficient by this time at expressing deep feelings and concerns but may have no idea at all how to make small talk at a party. In order to feel comfortable and successful in different kinds of relationships, the patient might need to work on developing such skills as trust and intimacy, anger management, and assertiveness. Even if the patient no longer holds anger in until she explodes, that doesn't mean that she knows how to handle a confrontation gracefully or when it might be better to walk away. Many of her ways of dealing with people up to this point have been trauma-based, and those old ways need to be replaced with new skills.

As the patient is beginning to deal with the tasks of the third phase, however, remember that the phases of therapy don't have neat dividing lines. Even in the midst of the third phase, it's not unusual for unprocessed memories or BASK components to pop up, which means falling back on the tools for containment and processing. As I often tell patients, I've become convinced the cosmos is arranged such that we do not run out of stuff to work on in this lifetime. It's important for both patients and therapists to understand this is a normal part of the therapy, so they don't see it as having failed or slipped backward.

Unlike the work described in the previous chapters, I don't have unique tools for the third phase. This is the kind of therapy that most mental health practitioners are trained to do. However, there are many excellent books and resources available for therapists to recommend to patients or for patients to read on their own that will help with the tasks of the final phase.

One resource you might find helpful is my other book, *Healing Everyday Traumas: Free Yourself from the Scars of Bullying, Criticism and Other Old Wounds* (2022). In it, I've described a variety of conventional tools useful for containment, centering, emotional regulation and memory processing. These include breathing exercises, mindfulness, memory reconsolidation, and finding "glimmers" (a way to lessen the negativity bias of protectors and the critical voice). There are also more extensive descriptions of the critical voice, as well as the energy psychology exercises you'll find in Chapter 13 of this book.

Another helpful book is *Self-Esteem* by McKay and Fanning (2000), which I mentioned in Chapter 6. It contains exercises to help with many important skills, such as handling mistakes, responding to criticism, being assertive, and even raising emotionally healthy children.

The concept of boundaries can be difficult to grasp, and even therapists sometimes have a hard time explaining it. Oftentimes we walk away from an interaction from someone feeling uncomfortable, distressed or just plain "icky" without realizing that the problem is that our boundaries have just been violated. Katherine's (1991) book *Boundaries: Where You End and I Begin* does a good job of defining the concept and giving examples to illustrate it, so that people can recognize when boundary violations occur. Her sequel (2000), *Where to Draw the Line,* gives many specific examples of both healthy and unhealthy boundaries around a variety of subjects and contexts — there are chapters on boundaries related to anger, possessions, divorce, and so on. Even though these are older works, they've stood the test of time.

Dialectical Behavior Therapy (DBT) is a therapeutic approach specifically designed for the treatment of borderline personality disorder, not dissociative disorder. However, many trauma specialists now believe that almost all psychological disorders — including borderline personality disorder — are trauma-based, and I find that some of the techniques of DBT can work with patients with other diagnoses as well. In particular, Linehan's (2019) workbook *Skills Training Manual for Treating Borderline Personality Disorder* has a variety of exercises on such areas as mindfulness, distress tolerance, and emotion regulation that can be quite helpful. Even better, the exercises are arranged in handout format, making it easy for the therapist to photocopy them for patient use, if the patient doesn't have her own copy of the book.

A classic work on assertiveness training that many patients still enjoy is *When I Say No, I Feel Guilty* (Smith, 1975). The author teaches several specific assertiveness skills and then discusses how to apply them to different kinds of situations (dealing with spouse, dealing with boss, etc.). One example of his techniques is persistence, which therapists often refer to as the "broken record" technique. If you come from the CD era — or beyond — and have never heard a broken record, what happens when you have a record with a crack or a bad scratch in it is that the same short phrase of music plays over and over again until someone moves the phonograph needle. It doesn't get aggravated or frustrated, it doesn't get any louder or more intense — it just repeats the same words and tones until someone fixes it. My more up-to-date image is the "GPS lady." If the GPS tells you to turn left and you blow right through the intersection, she doesn't yell at you, "You idiot! You were supposed to turn left!" Instead, she calmly says, "Recalculating [pause]. At the next intersection, make a U-turn...." Being able to persist in stating your case without losing your cool is a valuable interpersonal skill. The book contains many other concepts and techniques that the patient can work on as well, especially with the therapist's help, to strengthen her ability to be assertive.

Many patients arrive in therapy having never had a truly healthy relationship. If a person has never had one, it's difficult even to imagine what one looks and feels like, let alone to put it into practice. An excellent reference on this subject is Page's (2013) book *Happily Married: The 8 Essential Traits of Couples Who Thrive*. It's written in clear language with specific examples and covers such topics as commitment, goodwill, communication, and intimacy. For patients already in committed relationships, it helps them articulate what's good about the relationship and what perhaps needs to change. For patients who are on their own but looking for new partners, it helps them know what to look for, so that they'll be able to recognize healthy relationship skills in other people when they find them.

These books are only a few examples; there are many other resources that can be found for both therapists and patients. When a patient comes in with a new informational book and asks me whether I think she should read it, I almost always say yes, as long as it doesn't seem likely to be triggering beyond her ability to deal with it. I explain that it can be very useful to listen to other opinions, even when it turns out that we disagree with them. Thinking about what we *don't* believe often helps us to clarify and articulate what we *do* believe, in ways that we couldn't before. As a side benefit, it may also help the patient give herself permission to disagree with something said by an "authority."

The Issue of Leaving Therapy

In addition to the tasks mentioned above, there is one other major issue that will need to be resolved in the final phase: termination, or finishing therapy. Actually, there are at least two important issues intertwined in this task: the fear of "leaving the nest" and flying on one's own, and the grief of leaving the therapist.

If the therapy proceeds well—if the therapist is able to establish warmth and rapport, and the patient is able to build trust—it's normal for the patient to become emotionally dependent on the therapist, at least to some degree. This is a healthy development if the therapist is also mindful of helping the patient to grow beyond it. As part of the larger task of becoming emotionally independent, then, there's the more specific task of resolving the fears of not having access to the therapist's guidance, support and encouragement. As a practical matter, once the fears have been acknowledged, honored, and addressed, this is often accomplished by allowing the patient to wean off therapy gradually—by changing from once a week to every other week, then once a month, then perhaps once every few months on an "as needed" basis. That allows the patient to "try her wings" safely, until she has confidence she can indeed make it on her own.

Before this transition can be accomplished, however, the feelings it brings up will have to be addressed. Once the therapeutic relationship is well established, the thought almost inevitably occurs to the patient that someday it's going to end. She begins to anticipate the grief and fear she expects to feel when that happens. These feelings can crop up at any time in the course of therapy, and they often manifest as getting stuck or bogged down in the work. When the "stuckness" is explored, what the therapist and patient often find is a fear of getting well.

While honoring the fear, the image I like to give patients is that working in therapy is like climbing a series of steep hills or mountains. Most of the time, the traveler can only see what's behind her and a little way ahead. Only when she reaches the crest of one of the hills can she see a greater vista — and even that may be only to the crest of the next mountain. And no matter how much she's heard or read about the ocean, she can't truly know what it's like until she's crested the last slope and seen it for herself.

Just like that traveler, a person who has never felt joy can at best only dimly imagine what it's like until she experiences it for herself. In the same way, she can't imagine not needing to see and talk to her therapist on a frequent basis.

As her therapist, I know it can be a terrifying prospect. But I'm like a guide who has been over this particular mountain range and has seen the ocean on the other side. I can assure her, as often as needed, that it *is* there. As impossible as it may seem, I assure her, there will come a time when *she* decides (and I agree!) that she has other, better things to do with her time than to sit in my office and talk to me.

The Ultimate Goal of Therapy

There's one more important issue with particular relevance to patients with DID that may need to be resolved in the third phase, if it hasn't already been addressed. It has to do with the phenomenon of integration. When a dissociated part is integrated, it means the core re-owns the part and all of the memories and abilities it holds. It's no longer experienced as a separate entity but rather as an aspect of the core's own identity.

At some point, a DID patient will almost always ask me whether complete integration is my goal for the therapy. The question sometimes comes up in the initial interview, before we've even committed to working together, and sometimes arises only late in the therapy, toward the end of the second phase. I tell patients that integration isn't *my* goal, my rule about where the therapy has to go. However, I do believe that's the direction everyone moves in as they become healthier and stronger.

Whether we have DID or not, we all have different parts and aspects. We all play a variety of different roles in our lives. We're sons or daughters, brothers or sisters, spouses, partners, parents, and members of our communities. We go to work, to social gatherings, to religious services, to school, and to the gym. It's been my observation, over many years of clinical work, that the more mentally healthy we become, the more centered and integrated we also become. When we're not well centered — when the self who goes to work is very different from the self who hangs out with friends, for example — it can be difficult to move between roles. If we have to change from one to another more quickly than usual, it can feel jerky and disconnected — like stripping the gears on a car with manual transmission. If it were possible for a person to be perfectly centered, on the other hand, she'd be truly *herself,* the same self, in each and every situation. Her behavior would be somewhat different, of course, depending on what was appropriate for each situation, but her essence would be the same.

Again, whether we have DID or not, we all have parts and aspects of ourselves from all of the ages we've been so far—and sometimes our behavior reflects that. A painful memory gets triggered, our normal level of maturity vanishes, and we find ourselves acting like children or adolescents. When a part is integrated, on the other hand, one thing that happens is that the core takes over whatever job the part used to handle. Let's say there's a teenage part whose job it is to handle confrontations by yelling. Eventually, the core develops her assertiveness skills to the point she no longer needs the teenager to deal with these situations, and the teenage essence can be integrated into the core. The positive aspects of that "adolescent-ness" will still be there—a touch of brash rebelliousness, perhaps. But the patient's behavior during a confrontation will be coming from the core's repertoire of healthy, adult skills, not from the trauma-based responses of the teenager. If it were possible for a person to clear every bit of trauma—see my earlier comment about running out of stuff in this lifetime—then all of her parts and aspects would be integrated into the one, centered whole. She would still have the child qualities of curiosity and playfulness and the adolescent qualities of enthusiasm and idealism, but all of her responses, all of her decisions and actions, would be mediated through the healthy, balanced adult.

We all also have aspects of ourselves—thoughts, feelings, impulses—that we don't like and don't want to accept. Oftentimes we deny and dissociate these aspects, pushing them down into our subconscious, into what Carl Jung called the shadow. An important part of healing is finding the courage to face what's in our shadow, bring it into the light, and accept it as part of ourselves.

For most of us, becoming more centered feels wonderful. We feel more present, more authentic, more balanced. As we re-own our shadow side, we can also feel the increase in self-acceptance, serenity, and general well-being. Healing our own wounds even makes room for us to be more compassionate toward others.

For a patient with DID, however, the feelings may be much more mixed. As her traumas are processed and the memory parts integrated, the DID patient can certainly feel the relief as her symptoms abate and the deep satisfaction, even joy, that comes with healing. However, some of the other parts may have been the patient's closest companions since early childhood. In some cases, the patient may feel that these parts are her only friends, or at least the only ones who can be trusted. When she contemplates the prospect of integrating these parts, it may feel as if her best friends are all going to die. A task of the third phase, then, may be to help the DID patient deal with the anticipated grief over the loss.

There's a particular image that many of my DID patients have found comforting in this context. Remember that parts can't die, so instead of perceiving integration as a death, imagine that there's a river with many small streams flowing into it. Once a stream has joined the river, the water molecules are mixed together, so that it becomes impossible to tell which source a particular drop came from. But not one drop is lost. All of the qualities and talents and skills that were held by the part are still there. The only difference is that they're once again owned by the core and freely available to her. And it's by no means unhealthy if, as a legacy from her parts, the core is able to find pleasure and entertainment in her own company.

Actually, there is one skill that may diminish temporarily just after integration. People with high dissociative talent, especially those with DID, are often amazingly good at multi-tasking, because different parts can handle different jobs at the same time. When the parts are no longer separate, it becomes much harder until the core figures out how to multi-task on her own. Until that happens, it may be important to the patient's physical safety for both therapist and patient to be aware of this issue and to work on adapting to the change.

CHAPTER 12

New Approaches to Treatment

To this point, we've covered in some detail the three phases of the treatment model that is the current standard of care for trauma treatment. I've also described a variety of visualization tools and other resources that can make the patient's process of working through the tasks of the various phases much safer and more comfortable.

In this chapter and the next, I'd like to acquaint you with a new set of tools that come from the field of energy psychology, a cousin of mind-body medicine. As I mentioned at the very beginning of the book, it's my experience that these powerful new techniques can be easily interwoven into the conventional three-phase model and that—when combined with good, traditional therapy by a knowledgeable and skillful therapist—can significantly enhance the effectiveness of the therapeutic process.

For clinicians who aren't familiar with energy psychology, this chapter talks about what this field is and how it developed from ancient roots. Lay readers who like to know the hows and whys of things may be curious about it, too. If this doesn't especially interest you, though, feel free to skip or skim this chapter and go on to the next, which gets into the actual energy psychology techniques.

Psychologist Roger Callahan (2000) told a fascinating anecdote about a patient he called Mary. Around 1980, they were working together on her intense, life-long phobia of water. He'd been working with her for about a year and had tried every conventional therapy he could think of. She'd gotten a little better, but not much. One day, as they were working in sight of a swimming pool, she became very upset and complained of an "awful feeling" in the pit of her stomach. Callahan had been studying Chinese medicine and had learned that one of the end points of the stomach meridian is at the bone just underneath each eye. With some desperation, he suggested she tap on these points to see if that would quiet the stomach upset. After about two minutes, she exclaimed that it was gone. It turned out that she meant not only the stomach upset but the entire phobia as well. She was immediately able to dabble her hands in the pool and splash water on her face with no difficulty. Later that night, she went to the beach and waded out waist-deep into the ocean. Even more astonishing, as of the writing of Callahan's book in 2000, her phobia had never returned.

The Field of Energy Psychology

That incident marked the beginning of the modern field of energy psychology. Energy psychology is closely allied to the concepts of mind-body medicine. The mind-body approach has become increasingly popular in recent years, but for centuries before that, traditional Western medicine preferred to act as if the mind and the body were completely separate entities and could successfully be treated without reference to each other. "Physical" ailments were the province of internists, surgeons, and other medical specialists, while "mental" illnesses were treated by psychiatrists, psychologists and psychotherapists.

If you stop to think about it, though, you'll see how absurd this distinction is. We're all aware of ways our mental and emotional processes affect our physical being. The fact is that every mental event (thought, feeling, perception, etc.) that you experience is registered in the form of physical (biochemical and electrical) changes in your brain. In turn, these changes in the brain may trigger a whole sequence of changes in the rest of the body. For example, most people have experienced the distinctive feeling of an adrenaline "rush" after being suddenly frightened. Anxiety may bring on the sensation of "butterflies" in the stomach. Sadness can cause tears and a lump in the throat. All of these are simple examples of mental/emotional events having physical consequences.

Another kind of example is biofeedback. No one knows exactly how biofeedback works, but it's clear that it does. An average person with no special expertise can sit down in front of a machine and, with the help of the feedback it provides, can learn to use mental imagery, muscle relaxation, controlled breathing or similar techniques to lower his heart rate or blood pressure—processes once thought to be completely outside the range of conscious control.

As you can see, mental and emotional events can create real physical reactions in the body. As it happens, the interaction occurs the other way around as well. It's easy to find instances of physical factors that create changes in people's mental and emotional experience. For example, many women experience "the blues" on the first day of their menstrual cycle because of the change in hormone levels. Medications and drugs are also a physical (chemical) factor. It's been found that taking medication to increase the level of the neurotransmitter serotonin in the brain is quite helpful for at least some people; they report feeling less depressed, even before they make any changes to their behavior or their circumstances. Psychiatrist Peter Kramer (1993) stirred up quite a controversy in his book *Listening to Prozac* when he noted that some people undergo a significant personality change while on this kind of medication, becoming more self-confident, outgoing and assertive. Many illegal drugs, and legal substances used inappropriately, cause euphoria. Excessive alcohol consumption affects the centers in the brain that have to do with good judgment and behavioral control, so that people do and say things that they otherwise wouldn't. Mind-body medicine is exploring ways in which mental/emotional interventions can foster physical health. Researchers are also looking at ways in which changes to our physical health, such as an improved diet, can have a positive effect on mood. We're learning more and more ways we can intervene from either direction to increase a person's overall health.

Energy psychology adds a third element to the mind-body paradigm: the energy field. It's been known for a long time by conventional science that every living being has a measurable energy field around it. Furthermore, we know from modern physics that matter and energy are interchangeable, that they're two expressions of the same thing. That's what Einstein's famous equation $E = mc2$ means: energy is equal to mass times the speed of light squared. Just as our physical being and our emotional being are intertwined and constantly interacting with each other, energy psychology suggests that our energy field is intertwined and interacting with our physical/emotional self. So, just as traditional medicine is learning it's possible to affect the physical level by treating the emotional level and vice versa, energy therapies seek to alleviate problems at the physical and emotional levels by effecting changes in the energy field.

As Callahan continued to develop his approach of applying energy concepts to psychological treatment, he concluded that the condition of our energy field is the *primary* determinant of our level of healthfulness. In his formulation, emotional problems and even some physical problems are merely symptoms of "perturbations," or disturbances, in our energy field. When those disturbances are cleared, the emotional and physical symptoms are alleviated or eliminated. Interestingly, this idea dovetails with current thinking in quantum physics. The current understanding is that matter and energy are not equally represented in the universe. It's been suggested, instead, that most of our universe is made up of energy and that matter is a specific exception. A more detailed explanation of the connections between established scientific principles and the concepts of energy psychology can be found in many sources, including Pert (1997), McTaggart (2008), Oschman (2015), and Church (2018).

The Historical Roots of Energy Psychology

One application of this concept you've probably heard about, and maybe even experienced for yourself, is acupuncture. Acupuncture was discovered at least 5,000 years ago in China, and perhaps even earlier than that elsewhere. According to the legend as related by Gallo (2000), soldiers fighting with stone knives and stone arrowheads discovered that if they were nicked slightly in certain places—but not just any place—on their bodies, old pain from previous injuries was actually relieved. This explanation is apocryphal, of course, but the idea is that these experiences led to the identification of the acupoints still used today. However they were discovered, a modern acupuncturist learns to place the needles with precision in these exact points to achieve the desired results. Modern science has confirmed the acupoints are not simply hypothetical constructs—they have measurably lower electrical resistance from points on the skin just a short distance away.

An even older form of energy therapy is Ayurvedic medicine. This tradition comes from India and may be as much as 8,000 years old. It's considered to be the oldest form of medicine still in practice today. The Ayurvedic approach incorporates modern medical practices such as medication and surgery, but it also includes such elements as nutrition, herbal supplements, meditation and aromatherapy, as well as treatment of the major energy centers of the body, called the chakras.

The concept of an energy field was recognized in ancient Western thinking as well. In Greece, both Pythagoras (from whom we get the Pythagorean Theorem in geometry) around 500 B.C. and Hippocrates (author of the Hippocratic Oath) around 400 B.C. believed in a concept of universal energy and the idea that such energy could be used to heal. As recently as the 1500s, scholars from Europe traveled to India to study Ayurveda. One such person was Paracelsus, who is considered to be the father of modern Western medicine (Florida Vedic College, 2001). Among other accomplishments, Paracelsus discovered magnesium and pioneered the use of chemicals and minerals in medicine. He also believed harmony between man and nature was necessary for health and made extensive use of Ayurvedic principles in his work.

This holistic approach — that mind, body, and energy field all interact with each other — thus goes back thousands of years. But not all ancient thinkers subscribed to this view. The idea that mind and body should be viewed as completely separate entities was also put forth by influential Greek philosophers, notably Plato and Aristotle, who made no mention of the energy field at all.

The most powerful influence for incorporating this split into Western thinking, though, with the subsequent loss of our concept of universal life energy, was probably René Descartes. Reasoning from his famous statement "I think, therefore I am," he concluded that mind and matter were different type of substances. Versions of dualism, as this philosophy is called, have dominated Western thinking ever since.

There may have been something of a secondary agenda behind this line of reasoning as well. Although best known as a mathematician and philosopher, Descartes was also very much interested in anatomy and physiology. In the 17th century, however, these subjects were difficult to study. The Church, which was very powerful at the time, strictly forbade the dissection of human bodies because the body was considered to be the temple of the soul. In some locations, one dissection was permitted each year, but only by a licensed anatomist and only on the body of an executed criminal. It's been suggested that Descartes, or perhaps some of his followers, presented the concept of dualism to Church leaders to argue for a loosening of these restrictions. Their idea was that the Church could retain its control of the soul and let medicine have the body, which, after all, was only made of clay. If this story is true, it's ironic this reasoning removed a major roadblock to the development of modern medicine — and at the same time set medicine on a false trail from which we're still recovering.

The Promise of Energy Psychology

Modern methods of energy psychology have been used by thousands of practitioners with tens of thousands of clients and patients worldwide for more than 40 years. There's a massive amount of clinical data at this point indicating that — in the hands of well-trained, ethical therapists — these methods are safe and often amazingly effective. Callahan (1985) was laughed at—and worse—for what he called his "five-minute phobia cure," but it really is possible in many cases to reduce or eliminate a simple phobia in as little as 20 or 30 minutes.

We have much more than clinical data as well. During the last few decades, more than 155 studies using energy psychology techniques have been published in peer-reviewed journals. More than 80 of these studies were randomized controlled trials (considered the gold standard of research). There have also been more than 75 other pre- to post-treatment outcome studies, nine systematic reviews of energy psychology modalities, 15 reviews comparing these types of modalities with other therapies, 19 case studies or case series, and 64 theoretical articles. Of the clinical studies, 99 percent reported statistically significant positive results. Of the 79 studies that included follow-up investigations, 77 reported that the benefits were sustained for as much as 12 months. Three fMRI studies have documented neurological changes after energy psychology interventions (Association for Comprehensive Energy Psychology, 2022). One energy psychology method, Thought Field Therapy, has been recognized as an evidence-based practice for trauma, and others may follow soon. You can learn about the current research on energy psychology—and much more—by visiting the website of the Association for Comprehensive Energy Psychology (ACEP), www.energypsych.org.

Cognitive behavioral therapy, or CBT, is currently considered the gold standard in psychotherapy. I practiced CBT for many years—and still do. Energy psychology doesn't replace traditional therapy for its practitioners but adds another whole dimension to it. In my experience, CBT by itself has a major fallacy: the idea that if a person learns to identify and correct her "thinking errors," her negative emotions will be corrected as well. What CBT really seems to do is to teach the person how to *manage* her negative thoughts and feelings so they don't control her every waking moment. That's an improvement, but it's not a cure. Psychologists are taught never to talk in terms of cures.

Merely talking about a trauma rarely changes or heals it. When we talk about a painful event, it's as if we rip ourselves open and spread our guts out on the table. Then, if there's no healing or transformation that follows, we wind up stuffing it all back in. But now, we not only still have the original trauma, we also have a secondary layer of retraumatization. The more times we try to open the memory, the more layers of trauma we may develop around it. In fact, I think that much of patients' resistance to opening up in psychotherapy often comes from just this kind of experience, and we've all felt it at one time or another.

Energy psychology methods, when added to more traditional approaches, can be used effectively to treat both feelings and beliefs arising from past or present events. Experientially, when a painful memory is "cleared," what it feels like is that the emotional charge is completely removed. The person can still remember what happened, but the event no longer has hurt or fear or anger connected with it. Furthermore, as Callahan's example of Mary demonstrates, our experience over the past 25 years is that, once a memory is cleared of its emotional charge using energy psychology methods, it stays cleared.

At least some clearing can be obtained by using the traditional method of systematic desensitization. This is the principle behind the Healing Room exercise described in Chapter 10, and it does work. However, processing memories with our older, conventional tools can be a very long and tedious business. Research comparing different approaches has found that energy methods are almost always considerably faster (Feinstein, 2019). Using desensitization to clear even a single-incident trauma, such as a car accident, could take as many as six to ten sessions to thoroughly clear all of the elements of the event. With energy methods, it may be possible to clear a single-incident trauma in as little as one or two sessions. I've also found energy methods to have a much lower chance of flooding (triggering the whole memory to come flooding back in all at once and at full intensity) and retraumatization.

Types of Energy Psychology Approaches

Based on what Callahan had learned from Chinese medicine, chiropractic, yoga, and various other fields and what he had observed from Mary, he went on to develop a method he called Thought Field Therapy. Since then, many other techniques and therapies have been developed that also fall under the heading of energy psychology. Many practitioners believe there are actually several interrelated energy systems, but the three that are the most commonly used are the *meridians*, the *chakras*, and the *biofield.* Some treatment modalities address more than one of these systems. However, the best known of the energy psychology modalities tend to use just one energy system and can be grouped roughly according to which system is their major focus.

Meridian-Based Methods

Many cultures around the globe describe some concept of universal energy or life energy. In traditional Chinese medicine, this energy is called *chi* or *qi* (pronounced "chee"). You may already be familiar with this word, if you've ever studied Tai Chi or Qi Gong. Practitioners of Chinese medicine believe that chi flows along pathways in the body called meridians. There are thought to be hundreds of meridians, but 12 or 14 are considered major pathways. Each of the major meridians is associated with a particular organ system in the body and with certain emotions. The theory is that problems are caused by blockages that prevent energy from flowing smoothly through the body. Treating the meridians removes the blockages and therefore alleviates the problems.

The acupoints mentioned earlier are located on these meridians, like towns along a roadway. Unlike the acupoints, the meridians are hypothetical—that is, there's no obvious anatomical structure we can point to, as we could with a nerve or a blood vessel. It's been suggested they may run through the body's interstitial connective tissue (Fung, 2009; Langevin and Yandow, 2000). Whether the theory about chi flowing along the meridians turns out to be supported or not by future research, all meridian-based methods treat problems by stimulating the acupoints.

Remember that the acupoints *do* have a basis in physical reality; they are points on the skin that are identifiable by their lower electrical resistance. With acupuncture, the practitioner stimulates these points with needles, but energy psychology methods use acupressure—that is, by having the patient tap, rub or hold the points herself. Stimulating the acupoints on a particular meridian is believed to rebalance the energy field as a whole and to treat problems related to that meridian. For example, the stomach meridian is also associated with the emotions of anxiety and obsessive worry; when Callahan's patient Mary rebalanced her stomach meridian by tapping on the end points under her eyes, she not only resolved her stomach symptoms but her anxiety as well. One essential element of this kind of treatment seems to be to "activate" the problem or issue to be worked on—in other words, to get the particular neurons connected with the memory to fire—by turning one's conscious attention to one or more of its BASK components.

Callahan's Thought Field Therapy, or TFT, is an example of a meridian-based method. To treat a particular problem, such as anger, a TFT practitioner teaches the client to use an algorithm—that is, to tap on certain acupoints in a certain order.

Another example of a meridian-based method is Gary Craig's (1999) Emotional Freedom Techniques, or EFT. Craig, a businessman who became a performance coach and motivational speaker, originally studied under Callahan. After learning TFT, however, he began to question some of the tenets of this method. After trying out a number of variations, Craig concluded there was no harm done by tapping on more acupoints than were actually required for a given problem. Instead of having to learn dozens of algorithms, one could simply tap on or near the endpoints of all 12 meridians every time. Another question he explored had to do with the ordering of points to be used. Again, after trying it out in practice, he concluded it wasn't necessary to tap the points in any particular order. These changes have made EFT a much simpler method to learn than TFT, even for nonprofessionals. Many people without any specialized training are able to use these techniques on themselves to address a variety of mild to moderate emotional and even physical symptoms. One of the self-help books based on Craig's techniques is Arenson's *Five Simple Steps to Emotional Healing* (2001).

Another variation on EFT is a method called Choices, which was developed by psychologist Patricia Carrington (2001). What makes this method different from basic EFT is that it not only seeks to clear a negative emotion or belief but to instill a healthy, positive alternative, all within the same procedure.

Chakra-Based Methods

The concept of the chakras comes from ancient Indian tradition. Various traditions differ in the number of chakras they include; the formulation probably best known in Western culture describes seven major ones. These chakras are thought to be the major energy centers of the body, located along the midline of the body from the base of the spine to the top of the head.

One example of a chakra-based method is Advanced Integrative Therapy. Developed by psychotherapist Asha Clinton (2006), AIT isn't simply a set of techniques but a complete system of psychotherapy integrating transpersonal, body-centered and psychodynamic perspectives. It's used to treat traumatic experiences and their aftereffects, including negative feelings and beliefs, destructive desires and fantasies, obsessions, compulsions, and physical symptoms. And because people often experience repeated traumas that share a common theme — such as abandonment, humiliation or betrayal — AIT is designed to treat not only individual traumas, but whole traumatic patterns or themes.

One important contribution from AIT is the idea that a traumatic experience results in not only one negative belief, but a *matrix* of related and interconnected beliefs. A matrix on inadequacy, for example, might include such items as "I am inadequate," "I can never do anything right," and "I'll never be good enough." Each of these beliefs is just distinct enough that clearing one won't necessarily take the steam out of any of the others. In order to fully resolve the problem, it's necessary to identify and clear all of the elements contributing power to the matrix. In AIT, the treatment of a belief matrix also includes instilling a healthy, realistic alternative to each negative belief that's cleared. For the belief "I can never do anything right," the healthy alternative might be "I can do many things quite well enough."

The major advantage of a meridian-based method such as EFT is that patients can often learn it in one session and can use it on themselves between sessions for homework. The major limitation of many meridian-based methods like EFT is that it's usually necessary to be very specific in choosing what to focus on. If the patient is working in session on clearing the memory of a car accident, for example, she might need to focus on each individual piece, or aspect, of the memory separately—the sound of the squealing tires, the image of the other car barreling toward her, the feeling of powerlessness, the force of the impact, the fear for her daughter's safety, and so on. In contrast, the chakra-based methods such as AIT tend to be much more detailed and complicated even for practitioners to learn, let alone patients. But many therapists who practice both types of methods have found chakra-based methods are more powerful, often allowing an entire traumatic experience to be cleared at one time.

Biofield Methods

The biofield is the multi-layered energy field surrounding and permeating the physical body. All energy methods are thought to treat the biofield in one way or another. What distinguishes the methods in this category is the focus on the biofield as a whole rather than on the acupoints or the chakras.

One example of a biofield method is Reiki, developed by Mikao Usui (International Center for Reiki Training, 2007). Reiki practitioners are thought to channel healing energy to wherever the patient needs it by putting their hands on or near the patient's body. Other methods in this category include Therapeutic Touch (Krieger, 1979) and Healing Touch (Hover-Kramer, 2002). These two methods are most widely known among nurses and other health professionals, especially in hospital settings, where they've often been used to relieve pain and anxiety, to increase relaxation, and to promote healing.

As with any medical or health procedure, it's important to seek out practitioners who are well trained, competent, and ethical. If you were planning to have plastic surgery, it would be a good idea to look for a doctor who's board certified in that specialty. Similarly, licensed mental health practitioners are required to have specified courses of training, to participate in continuing education, and to subscribe to the ethical codes of their respective disciplines. If you have a history of serious psychological trauma or dissociative disorder, I'd strongly encourage you to look for a therapist who has specialized training in these areas beyond graduate school. Not all clinicians are equally knowledgeable about or skilled in the treatment of trauma and dissociation. In addition, the Association for Comprehensive Energy Psychology (www.energypsych. org) has instituted a certification program for energy practitioners. Through this website, it's possible to identify practitioners who are both licensed in their conventional disciplines (psychology, social work, etc.) and certified in the modality called Comprehensive Energy Psychology. Many of the individual energy methods each have defined levels of certification as well.

With the continuing development of these new tools, and in the hands of careful and competent practitioners, the future of trauma treatment looks promising indeed.

In the next chapter, I'll teach you how to use a variety of simple energy psychology techniques. One technique is a set of exercises for energy hygiene. The second is a meridian-based form of "tapping." Under this heading, I've included a version of EFT. The third is a chakra-based method, in this case a technique called Breathing the Chakras.

CHAPTER 13

Energy Psychology
Techniques

Balancing the Energy Field: Energy Hygiene

Physician Robert Becker (1985) helped establish that the energy field of every living being has polarity — much the same way that a magnet has north and south poles. Under various conditions, the polarity of the field can become reversed, or the field can become nonpolarized or disorganized. One could easily fill another book describing these conditions and their consequences in detail. However, it's sufficient for our purposes to understand that all of these conditions undermine the effectiveness of energy techniques (and probably traditional therapies as well). It may seem that a technique isn't working at all, or you may see an improvement but find it doesn't last.

When I'm working with patients directly, I actually test for these conditions. If needed, I apply specific corrections for specific conditions. But most people are able to create a beneficial effect by doing a series of these corrective exercises themselves.

These exercises have no negative side effects, so there's no harm in doing them even if you don't need them. (Think of it like putting a band-aid on healthy skin. It's not needed, but it's not hurting anything, either.) There's no limit to how often you can use them, so many people build them into their schedule once or twice a day as a healthy routine. When done regularly, this practice is often referred to as energy hygiene.

The following is a set of energy hygiene exercises I often recommend to patients. You can pick and choose which ones you like, but doing the entire set usually takes less than 10 minutes. You can also do them in any order.

1. Tap the **side of hand point** 10 to 20 times. (This point is located on the side of the hand away from the thumb, even with the upper crease of the palm, just below the little finger knuckle.)

2. Rub the **neurolymphatic reflex points** for 10 to 15 seconds. (To find these points, go to the notch in your collarbone. Come down about 3 to 4 inches, then out about 3 inches to each side. Poke firmly around those areas until you find a spot on either or both sides that feels a bit tender.)

3. Rub or tap the **collarbone points** for 20 seconds or longer while breathing in through the nose and out through the mouth. For even better effect, cross your hands over to the opposite sides of your body. (These points are on the underside of the

collarbone, just off the breastbone on each side, in the hollow where the collarbone and breastbone meet. The easiest way to find this point is to raise your shoulders and feel for the hollows where the collarbone and breastbone meet.)

4. Butterfly Hug: Cross your forearms over your chest, allowing your hands to rest on the hollows of your shoulders. Gently pat with your hands, alternating sides.

5. Over Energy Correction (Left Side)[3]:

   a. Clasp your hands and notice which thumb is on top. If your left thumb is on top, follow these directions... If your right thumb is on top, use the Right Side version below.) .

   b. Cross your left ankle over your right.

   c. With your arms outstretched in front of you, put your hands back to back (palms facing outward).

   d. Cross your right wrist over your left.

   e. Interlace your fingers.

   f. Circle your hands down and then inward, resting your interlaced fingers on your chest.

   g. On the in-breath, touch your tongue to the roof of your mouth; on the out-breath, let your tongue fall naturally to the floor of your mouth.

   h. Continue for 90 seconds or longer.

---

3 The exact origins of the Over Energy Correction and the Cross Crawl seem to have been lost in the mists of time. In the interests of giving credit where it's due, however, I'd particularly like to acknowledge the contributions of Roger Callahan, Wayne Cook, Paul and Gail Dennison, Fred Gallo, George Goodheart, Steven Rochlitz, and John Thie.

    i. Optional: Repeat the exercise in the opposite direction.

6. Over Energy Correction (Right Side)

    a. Clasp your hands and notice which thumb is on top. If your right thumb is on top, follow these directions.

    b. Cross your left ankle over your right.

    c. With your arms outstretched in front of you, put your hands back to back (palms facing outward).

    d. Cross your left wrist over your right.

    e. Interlace your fingers.

    f. Circle your hands down and then inward, resting your interlaced fingers on your chest.

    g. On the in-breath, touch your tongue to the roof of your mouth; on the out-breath, let your tongue fall naturally to the floor of your mouth.

    h. Continue for 90 seconds or longer.

    i. Optional: Repeat the exercise in the opposite direction.

7. Cross Crawl:

    a. While standing, lift your left knee (as if marching) and at the same time lift your right arm and swing it across the midline of your body. Touch your outer left thigh with your right hand.

    b. Return to standing position.

    c. Lift your right knee while lifting and swinging your left arm across your body. Touch your outer right thigh with your left hand.

  d. Repeat this sequence for 60 seconds or more.

  e. Optional: add humming or simple math (e.g., count upward by 3s).

  f. This exercise can also be done sitting or lying down.

It may also help to add a breathing exercise before, during or after the energy hygiene exercises. Virtually any form of controlled breathing will work, but one simple one is the 4-3-7 technique (Eldringhoff, 2014). It's also easy to remember, because $4 + 3 = 7$. Breathe in through your nose for a count of four, feeling your belly expand so that you know you're getting a good, full breath. Hold for a count of three, then breathe out through your mouth for a count of seven. The cadence is about one count per second. It's

---

PLEASE NOTE: As a trauma specialist, my experience is that energy psychology techniques, such as the two techniques that follow, can be used to heal even the most severe forms of trauma. Many of the people reading this book are here because they have histories of such trauma. However, **this depth of healing is not something to attempt on your own.** It should be done together with a skilled, licensed therapist who has specialty training in trauma treatment and in the use of energy psychology techniques for trauma. In the meantime, though, these techniques can be used to great effect for centering, calming and being fully present in real time. They can also be used to help you cope with present-day challenges, such as letting go of the frustration of dealing with a difficult co-worker.

---

been known for over a hundred years that chronic shallow breathing can contribute to exhaustion and irritability. More recently, it's been shown that breathing exercises can be used to help counteract the effects of stress. It also appears the long, controlled exhale may be even more effective than the controlled inhale at disengaging from the fight/flight stress response and stimulating the relaxation response.

If you have time to do only one of these exercises, I recommend the Over Energy Correction. In particularly stressful times, you might set your watch or phone to ding on the hour and then do this exercise for one to two minutes every hour throughout the day.

Meridian Tapping

There are now hundreds of energy psychology techniques in the literature. By far the best known at this point is the one called Emotional Freedom Techniques, or EFT. Gary Craig created the first version of EFT, but there are now many variations on his original approach. The version presented here is similar to the way Craig was teaching it in 2000, but with some of my own spin as well.

As I mentioned earlier, EFT is a meridian therapy. This type of technique is often called acupressure, because it uses several of the same points on the body as acupuncture but stimulates those points with gentle tapping rather than needles. There are several hundred acupoints all over the body. Craig chose to use particular points because they're at or near the endpoints of the major meridians. The basic idea is that tapping on these points stimulates the flow of energy along the meridians.

The Acupressure Points Most Commonly Used

Before you can begin using a meridian technique, you need to know where the tapping points are. The technique will work even if you're slightly off the point, but the more precise you are, the better. The points are quite small, so I recommend tapping with the first two fingers of either hand to maximize the odds of hitting the points. Most of the points are symmetrical on both sides of the body. On several of them, you can tap with both hands at the same time. On the rest of them, you can tap first with one hand, then switch and tap with the other. Many practitioners believe that tapping on both sides of the body is more effective than tapping only on one side.

The locations of the points are as follows (and see diagram on page 148):

- Eyebrow: at the beginning of the eyebrow, just off the bridge of the nose
- Side of eye: at the corner of the eye, on the bone
- Under eye: on the top of the bone, just under the center of the eye
- Under nose: on the center just above the upper lip
- Under lip: in the hollow of the chin
- Collarbone: on the underside of the collarbone, just off the breastbone (the easiest way to find this point is to raise your shoulders and feel for the hollows where the collarbone and breastbone meet)
- Underarm: on the side of the body, about four finger widths (around three inches) below the bottom of the armpit

- Thumb: on the side of the thumb away from the fingers, even with the base of the nail
- Index finger: on the side of the index finger away from the other fingers, even with the base of the nail
- Middle finger: same place on the middle finger
- Little finger: same place on the little finger
- Side of hand: on the side of the hand away from the thumb, even with the upper crease of the palm, just below the little finger knuckle
- Back of hand: in the hollow between the tendons of the ring finger and little finger, close to the knuckles

One more set of points will be useful to know. These are the neurolymphatic reflex, or NLR, points. Colloquially, they're known as the "sore spots" or "tender spots," because they're often tender to the touch. One way to find them is to go to the notch in your collarbone. Come down about three to four inches, then out about three inches to each side. Poke around those areas until you find a spot on each side that feels a bit tender. Note that the two NLR points can be asymmetrical, and they can be in slightly different locations at different times so even if you've done this many times before, you may have to hunt for them a bit. Sometimes you may find a spot only on one side; if so, then cross over and use the opposite hand. (Callahan, the developer of Thought Field Therapy, believed that the NLR on the left is more powerful than the one on the right.) Also note that the NLR points are much lower on the chest than the collarbone tapping points.

Diagrams on the next page provide an illustration of all of these points as well.

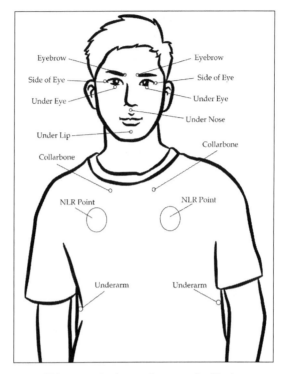

Diagram 1: Acupoints on the Body

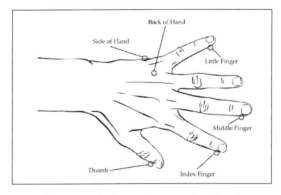

Diagram 2: Acupoints on the Hand

Using EFT Tapping for Centering

Tapping the acupoints — even with no particular problem in mind — can be quite soothing. (Other methods rub or hold the points instead of tapping on them, which can also be effective.) Research has found that stimulating the acupoints creates real, measurable changes in our neurochemistry. The fight/flight response is reduced and the relaxation response strengthened. Among other things, tapping increases the production of serotonin and the endorphins and helps to regulate the stress hormone cortisol.

The simplest way to begin trying out this exercise is to start at the eyebrow points and work your way down the whole chart, ending with the points on the fingers. You can tap as few or as many times as you like. As the process comes to feel more familiar, you can tap each point until your intuition tells you it feels "finished." Guided by your intuition, you can also choose to tap just some of the points, in any order. For someone with DID, though, the one caution (as always) is to check whether this change to the process is coming from your inner wisdom or from the protectors trying to sabotage it. When in doubt, stay with the process as written.

Using EFT Tapping to Clear a Problem

The procedure for using tapping to clear or reduce a problem is longer and more detailed. The full-length version of this technique has four steps, plus preparation and finishing.

Preparation. The first thing you need to do is decide what problem you want to work on. This problem is often referred to as the "target." If you're doing this as self-help, without the guidance of a therapist, please remember the caution I mentioned before: **focus on a problem or challenge in the present day, and one that's of only moderate intensity.** Ideally, it will be an issue that causes you discomfort but doesn't overwhelm you (or trigger significant trauma memories) when you think about it.

Targets can be many different kinds of things, but the easiest ones to pinpoint are a negative *feeling* or a negative *belief*. In the beginning, you may find it easier if you choose either a feeling or a belief as your target.

The task here is to think of a phrase or sentence that captures the essence of what you want to clear. For example, you might choose something like:

- my fear of flying
- my anxiety about giving this speech
- my anger at myself for the choice I made to take this job
- my belief that I need everyone to like me
- my belief that I'll never be good enough at this job

This is called the "reminder phrase." The more specific you are, the better this technique will work.

Using your reminder phrase to help you, focus on the problem as intensely as you can. On a scale from 0 to 10, where 0 is no feeling at all and 10 is extremely intense, decide how intense the problem is at this very moment.

Before you begin Step 1, do either the Over Energy Correction or the Cross Crawl. Either exercise will help to rebalance your energy field as a whole, and that's likely to make whatever healing technique you use more effective.

Step 1: Setting Up for the Healing. Find the NLR points ("sore spots") and rub them gently but firmly while saying the following three times with feeling:

> Even though I have [fill in with reminder phrase],
> I deeply and completely love and accept myself.

As an alternative, you may tap the side of hand point during the set-up instead of rubbing the NLR points.

By the way, you might notice that these two actions are the first and second energy hygiene exercises used during the setting-up step. What this does is to combine a traditional cognitive technique (the use of affirmations) with a technique that rebalances the energy field specifically around this issue. Experience has shown us that this combination is more powerful than simply repeating the words of an affirmation by itself.

Initially, your protectors (or the critical voice for a singleton) may make it seem impossible to say that you love and accept yourself. My recommendation is to use this affirmation if you possibly can, even if it doesn't feel true yet. If it's too much of a stretch, try "I deeply and completely accept myself" or "I know I'm doing the best I can" or "I truly like the person I'm becoming" or something similar. Push back against your protectors and make the strongest statement that you can.

Step 2: The Sequence. Focus on your reminder phrase. Add a verb such as "releasing" or "healing" at the beginning of the phrase, so it becomes a complete sentence—e.g., "I am completely releasing my anxiety." Tap on each of the acupoints about 7 to 9 times, or until the point feels "finished." In EFT, the custom is to say the phrase once at each point as you tap. Remember you can tap on the points on both sides of the body if you like:

Beginning of the eyebrow
Side of the eye
Under the eye
Under the nose
Hollow of the chin
Under the collarbone
Under the arm
Side of the thumb
Side of the index finger
Side of the middle finger
Side of the little finger
Side of the hand, at the crease

For the eyebrow, side of eye, under eye, collarbone, and underarm points, you can use both hands at the same time. For the other points, you can tap on just one side or alternate from side to side.

Step 3: The Nine Gamut Procedure. This is a brain-balancing exercise. The back of hand point (between the tendons for the ring and little fingers) is sometimes called the gamut point. Find this point and tap on it continuously while doing the following nine things (hence the name of the exercise):

1. Close your eyes
2. Open your eyes
3. Look hard down to one side (without moving your head)
4. Look hard down to the other side
5. Roll your eyes in a circle (without moving your head)
6. Roll your eyes in a circle the other direction
7. Hum or sing a few notes (not a song)
8. Count upward by 2s or 3s or do simple arithmetic
9. Hum or sing a few notes (not a song)

Step 4: Repeat the Sequence. Focus in again on the target and repeat your sentence, once at the beginning or at each point. Tap on each of the points as before, 7-9 times or until it feels "finished":

Beginning of the eyebrow
Side of the eye
Under the eye
Under the nose
Hollow of the chin
Under the collarbone
Under the arm
Side of the thumb
Side of the index finger
Side of the middle finger

Side of the little finger
Side of the hand, at the crease

Finishing. When you get to the end of the process, take a deep breath and exhale. Notice whether you're experiencing any emotions, memories, insights, or body sensations—if so, you may even want to jot them down. Now put them aside—or put them into the vault if need be—and turn your attention back to the original problem that you were working on. Focus just on that one target as you did at the beginning and again rate the intensity from 0-10.

After You Finish One Round of Tapping

After you've completed the four steps, the finishing phase includes noticing what happened to the intensity level of the problem. There are several possible outcomes, and what you do next will depend on which outcome you're experiencing. This isn't an exhaustive list, but here are some suggestions to consider.

If the intensity level is down to 0 or 1: Hooray! Allow yourself to tune in to the sense of relief and accomplishment of having cleared the issue. Consider whether there's a positive feeling or belief you'd like to strengthen. Many energy practitioners believe clearing an issue down to 0 is only half the process; it's equally important to replace the negative with a corresponding positive feeling, belief or skill. For example, if you were working on alleviating your anxiety over giving a speech, you could focus on increasing your feeling of confidence and calmness in that situation. To adapt the tapping technique for installing a positive, you could skip the set-up altogether or modify the wording to something like, "As I am strengthening my [fill in the desired state], I deeply and completely love and accept myself." Then go through the remaining steps just as you did before.

Once one issue is cleared, you might also want to check whatever feelings, memories, insights, etc., came up in the finishing phase (if any) to see if they give you ideas about what to choose for your next target.

If the intensity level is lower but not yet 0 or 1: Try repeating the process. Change the phrasing in the set-up to "Even though I still have some of my _____," and change the reminder phrase to "I am completely releasing any remaining _____."

If the intensity goes down in the first round or two but then seems to get stuck: Consider switching to the chakra technique described in the next section. Sometimes the most thorough way to clear an issue is to use more than one energy system.

If the intensity doesn't go down: One possibility is to take another look at your reminder phrase. Does it capture where the real power is? For example, let's say you were tapping on "my anxiety about making this speech." The initial intensity is an 8, and it still feels like an 8 after a round of tapping. But when you tune in more closely to your feelings, you might find that the anxiety isn't the main issue—the power is in your *fear that you'll look stupid*. If that's the case, you can tap all day on anxiety, and the rating won't budge because you're aiming at the wrong target. Alternatively, it may be that your anxiety was the best focus originally, but now the target has shifted to fear.

That's why it's important in the finishing phase to focus in and assess *the problem you were working on.* Otherwise it may feel as if you're not getting anywhere, when actually you've cleared one problem and have already moved on to something else without realizing it.

What if the intensity rating increases after a round of tapping? If this happens, it often means you're getting in touch with feelings the protectors had dissociated and tried to keep buried. As uncomfortable as it may feel in the moment, this is actually a good thing in the long run. Remember these feelings have been there all this time and have been affecting you, even if you didn't know it. Having them come to the surface means you can work on them and possibly even resolve them once and for all. If the intensity is higher but is still at a level you can tolerate, the best thing is usually to keep working on the issue with several more rounds of treatment. Oftentimes the intensity will crest like a wave and then, like a wave, begin to ebb until it flows away.

Finally, if you follow these various suggestions and the intensity of an issue stays high, it may be that you need more help with it than this exercise can provide. I recommend putting the issue in your containment box or vault and seeking out a therapist — preferably one who practices energy psychology — to help you further.

EFT Short Form

There's also an abbreviated form of EFT that may work for at least some issues. It may be worth trying first, especially if you've just run into the restroom to deal with something going on in the immediate moment and have a very short time to get a grip.

The short form consists of doing Step 1 (the set-up) and tapping on the first seven points of the sequence (eyebrow, side of eye, under eye, under nose, hollow of chin, collarbone). It then goes directly to the finishing process, leaving out Steps 3 and 4 (the Nine Gamut Procedure and Repeat the Sequence).

If you use the short form and the intensity level only goes down one or two points (or doesn't go down at all), try using the full-length EFT sequence.

A Few Additional Notes About Targets

Tapping (and the chakra technique described next) can also be used on physical symptoms and sensations and cravings, as well as other kinds of issues. As you become more experienced with this kind of work, you'll be able to expand how you apply it. For example, your target might be "my headache" or "my craving for sweets."

If you like this technique and find it useful, you might find it helpful to make a list of possible targets you want to work on. One way to do this is to use the Safe Place. Sit in your Safe Place in a mindful, calm state. Give it a few minutes and see what thoughts, feelings, or body sensations attract your notice and write them down. If you're ready to work on something right then, see if there's any one item that seems to come to the forefront in the present moment, and focus on that.

In EFT, the custom is to repeat the reminder phrase at each tapping point of the sequence so you stay tuned in to the target. If you find it sufficient, though, you could also choose to say the reminder phrase once at the beginning of the sequence to focus on the target and then simply stay tuned in to it as you proceed.

A Simple Chakra-Based Technique

According to ancient tradition, the chakras are the major energy centers running down the midline of the body. The chakras are much larger than the acupoints. The word "chakra" translates as "wheel," and they're described as spinning or swirling wheels of energy that permeate the physical body and extend out beyond it in both front and back.

There are some differences of opinion, but the traditions most familiar to Western culture describe seven major chakras, ranging from the top of the head to the floor of the torso. Their locations are as follows:

- Seventh (crown): at the top of the head
- Sixth (brow): at the center of the forehead
- Fifth (throat): at the hollow of the throat
- Fourth (heart): at the small dip in the breastbone (run your fingers lightly down your breastbone to find where it bends slightly inward)
- Third (solar plexus): over the solar plexus, midway between the bottom of the breastbone and the navel
- Second (sacral): at the lower abdomen, three to four finger widths below the navel
- First (root): in the perineal area at the underside of the torso and extending just slightly up the torso in both front and back

The diagram below depicts the locations as well.

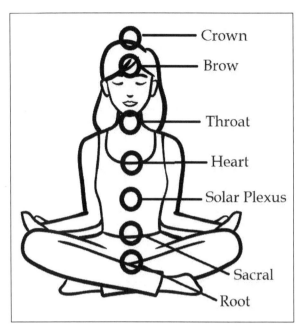

Diagram 3: Locations of the Chakras

Like the meridians, each chakra is thought to be associated with a part of the body and with certain emotions and needs. These emotions and needs will manifest differently depending on whether the chakra is balanced and clear or congested and out of balance. Knowing the psychological correlates of the chakras may help you identify which ones might benefit from extra attention as you apply a treatment technique:

- The **seventh chakra** is believed to be related to spirituality and idealism, as well as to issues about father and the masculine divine. When it's out of balance, you might experience apathy, disconnection from spirituality, or difficulty accepting new ideas.

- The **sixth chakra** has to do with knowledge, belief, intuition, insight and imagination. When it's congested, we tend to see confusion, lack of clarity, or a feeling of being stuck.

- The **fifth chakra** is associated with communication, self-expression and the ability to speak one's truth. Imbalance here might cause you to have difficulty expressing your thoughts and, especially, an inability to speak up for yourself.

- The **fourth chakra** is the heart center and has to do with love, caring, empathy and grief. When it's congested, it's associated with depression, jealousy, lack of forgiveness and a judgmental attitude.

- The **third chakra** is related to self-control and a sense of personal power and effectiveness. Imbalance may be experienced as low self-esteem, anger, frustration, shame and a feeling of powerlessness.

- The **second chakra** has to do with sexuality, self-concept and a sense of being productive. Congestion here is associated with guilt, blame, obsessiveness and difficulties with social skills.

- The **first chakra** is related to basic survival, safety, groundedness and courage, as well as to issues about mother and the feminine divine. Imbalance in this chakra may show up as insecurity, fear, stubbornness, lack of groundedness, or a lack of desire to survive.

Breathing the Chakras

This method, designed by psychotherapist Stephanie Eldringhoff and me, is a simple, elegant technique for clearing and balancing the chakras. It's easy to do and yet capable of producing a powerful effect. Another advantage of this technique is that it has a built-in process for strengthening a positive alternative to the target problem.

Before we go through the details of the technique, take a moment to think about the seven chakras listed above. Imagine that you can breathe through each of them, one at a time. The breath through the crown chakra goes up and down. The breath through the sixth, fifth, fourth, third, and second chakras goes in and out through both the front and back of the body. The breath through the root chakra goes both front and back and up and down. It may help to hold in mind the image of an accordion, with its bellows expanding and contracting. (Some people see the bellows expanding as they breathe in, others as they breathe out. You can choose whichever image works best for you.)

This technique starts in much the same way as the tapping technique in the previous section. The first thing to do is to choose what problem to work on. Refer to your list or use the Safe Place exercise, as before. Once you have a specific target in mind, tune into the problem as clearly and intensely as you can and give it an intensity rating from 0-10. Alternatively, you can simply notice the intensity of the issue in your body sensations. Then turn the reminder phrase into an action statement by adding a verb, such as "releasing" or "healing" — for example, "I am completely releasing my...."

Again parallel to the tapping technique, the next step is to do some form of setting up for the healing. You can use the same format as before: tap the side of hand point or rub the NLR points while saying the following three times:

> Even though I have [fill in with the problem], I deeply and completely love and accept myself.

From this point, do the following:

1. Focus on your seventh (crown) chakra and begin conscious breathing, as if the chakra has its own respiration. You can touch the chakra with one or both hands if it helps to sustain the focus. Repeat your action statement ("I am completely releasing my...") and take four conscious breaths, imagining the air flowing in and out in an up/down direction through the crown of your head. If your intuition tells you to take more than four breaths at any chakra, that's fine.

2. Turn your focus to your sixth (brow) chakra. Touch it with one or both hands if you like. Repeat your action statement and take four conscious breaths, imagining the air flowing in and out through the front and back of your head.

3. Repeat step 2 for the fifth, fourth, third, and second chakras, imagining the flow of air through the front and back of your body. At the first chakra, imagine the air flowing both front and back and up and down.

4. Pause and notice your feelings, thoughts and body sensations around the issue. See if anything else has come up as well. If so, set it aside for the moment. Recheck the intensity level of the issue you were working on.

After You Finish One Round of Breathing the Chakras

After you've completed a round of the chakra treatment, notice what happened to the intensity level of the problem and rate it using the 0-10 scale. The possible outcomes are the same as for the tapping exercise.

If the intensity level is down to 0 or 1: Hooray! Allow yourself to tune in to the sense of relief and accomplishment of having cleared the issue. Consider whether there's a positive feeling or belief you'd like to strengthen. As I mentioned earlier, many energy practitioners believe clearing an issue down to 0 is only half the process; it's equally important to replace the negative with a corresponding positive feeling, belief or skill. For example, if you were working on alleviating your anxiety over giving a speech, you could focus on increasing your feeling of confidence and calmness in that situation. The instructions for using Breathing the Chakras to install a positive alternative are in the next section.

Once one issue is cleared, you might also want to check whatever feelings, memories, insights, etc., came up in the finishing phase (if any) to see if they give you ideas about what to choose for your next target.

If the intensity level is lower but not yet 0 or 1: Try repeating the process. Change the phrasing in the set-up to

"Even though I still have some of my _____," and change the reminder phrase to "I am completely releasing any remaining _____."

If the intensity goes down in the first round or two but then seems to get stuck: Consider switching to the tapping technique described earlier. Sometimes the most thorough way to clear an issue is to use more than one energy system.

If the intensity doesn't go down: One possibility is to take another look at your reminder phrase. Does it capture where the real power is? Remember that the rating probably won't improve if you're aiming at the wrong target. Alternatively, it may be that the target has shifted to a something different. That's why it's important in the finishing phase to focus in and assess *the problem you were working on*. Otherwise it may feel as if you're not getting anywhere, when actually you've cleared one problem and have already moved on to something else without realizing it.

What if the intensity rating increases after a round of tapping? As you learned earlier, it often means you're getting in touch with feelings the protectors had dissociated and tried to keep buried. If the intensity is higher but is still at a level you can tolerate, the best thing is usually to keep working on the issue with several more rounds of treatment. Oftentimes the intensity will crest like a wave and then, like a wave, begin to ebb until it flows away.

Finally, remember this caution: if you follow these various suggestions and the intensity of an issue stays high, it may be that you need more help with it than this exercise can provide. I recommend putting the issue in your containment box or vault and seeking out a therapist – preferably one who practices energy psychology – to help you further.

Installing a Positive Alternative

If the intensity level is 0 to 1, it may be appropriate to work on cultivating a positive, desired state as an alternative to the problem state – a feeling, thought, action or physical response. Put that desired state into a statement such as "I am now feeling _____" or "I now believe _____" or "I will now do _____." Take a 0-10 rating of how strongly you resonate with this positive belief or desired state. (The rating will probably be a low number when you begin and will go up as you work on strengthening it.) Then continue the process as follows:

1. State your positive intention out loud. Turn your attention to your first chakra and take four conscious breaths, breathing through it front and back and down to the core of the earth. With each inhale, bring the healing state into the chakra, and with each exhale release anything that might remain of the problem state.

2. Turn your focus to your second (sacral) chakra. Touch it with one or both hands if you like. Repeat your positive statement and take four conscious breaths, imagining the air flowing in and out through the front and back of your body.

3. Continue the process in step 2 with the second through sixth chakras, breathing in and out both

the front and back of the chakra like an accordion. At the seventh chakra, let the breath go in and out in an up/down direction through the crown of your head.

4. Pause and notice your feelings, thoughts and sensations about both the target issue and your positive intention. Notice the degree to which you feel you've embodied the desired, positive alternative. Recheck the 0-10 rating you took before you started working on the positive state. If it's not yet a 10, you can do additional rounds to keep strengthening it until you feel complete resonance with it.

Consolidating the Gains

Whether you use tapping or the chakra technique to install a positive, it's helpful to choose a small action to take as soon as possible to support the new state. This action should be something opposite from the old problem state. Be alert for interference from your protectors that would sabotage you by setting an impossibly high goal. The chosen action can be as small as writing a note to put in your wallet or on your phone or leaving yourself a voice mail message to remind you of your new feelings and insights about the issue you worked on. If you have aromatic oils, you could put a drop on your skin and sniff it, then put another drop on a cotton ball and put it in a baggie to carry with you. When you sniff the scent again later, it will evoke the feeling of the healing experience.

By the way, there's no limit to the number of times per day that you can use any of these techniques. One colleague mentioned to me that she liked to do Breathing the Chakras every morning before she got out of bed. She found that it helped her feel centered and made an excellent start to the day.

EPILOGUE

A Note to Therapists
(and Patients)

Working with severely traumatized patients can be a very messy business, and it isn't everyone's cup of tea. Before you make the decision to work with these patients, you need to be aware of certain aspects of this kind of work. If you consider these aspects carefully, you may decide that this work just isn't for you. That's an excellent thing to know about yourself—no one is temperamentally suited to work with every possible type of patient. To know your own limits is a responsible, ethical decision, and one that deserves applause.

Working with severely traumatized patients is like doing therapy in a fishbowl. Every movement you make, every word you utter may be scrutinized and questioned. This is a reflection of the hypervigilance characteristic of PTSD. In order to maintain the patient's trust, you may find yourself having to be much more open and transparent about the therapy than usual. You'll need to be prepared to explain the hows and whys of each procedure you use. You may need to be able to adapt your techniques to work around trauma triggers, especially if your work involves physically touching the patient. It doesn't matter if the trigger seems insignificant or nonsensical to you; it has to be taken seriously and with a nonjudgmental attitude. At times, you'll also need to be open about your own process. That doesn't mean that you have to reveal a lot of personal details about your life, but it does mean owning what's going on with you in any given moment — when you lose focus or become distracted, for example. It's vital to be able to admit mistakes, without becoming defensive or trying to cover up. And if you tell a lie and are found out, the therapy, for all intents and purposes, is over.

If you choose to take on these kinds of patients, you have to be committed to doing your own work. This is true in any kind of therapy, but especially here. That doesn't mean that you have to have all of your issues resolved. The best expression of this point I ever heard was during my clinical training when, in some desperation, a student asked one of our professors, "Do you have to have all of your shit together before you can do therapy?" After thinking about it for a moment, the professor replied, "No, you don't have to have all of your shit together. But you do have to know where it is."

It's a very good thing that you don't have to have every problem resolved in order to do good therapy, or none of us would be able to work at all. As the professor pointed out, however, you do have to know your own stuff, because deep trauma work will inevitably bring it up one way or another. Most especially, you *must* be able to tell the difference between what is the patient's stuff and what is yours. On occasion, when a patient's issues hit too close to your own—e.g., both you and a prospective patient are going through painful divorces at the same time—you'll need to refer the patient out to someone else, or at the very least get help from peer consultation and your own therapist so that you aren't imposing your feelings, needs and issues on the patient.

Most therapists are familiar with the phenomenon of transference: when a patient has feelings about someone in her past—her father, for example—and projects those feelings onto the therapist. The feelings can be either positive or negative but, in either case, they don't actually belong to the therapist—they're being transferred from the original source. Dissociative patients, for obvious reasons, are likely to be more disconnected from their feelings than non-dissociative patients. As a result, they may be especially prone to transference. It may be even more important than usual to be alert for this phenomenon and prepared to explain it in nonjudgmental ways. When therapists experience the same phenomenon, it's called "countertransference." Because these patients are hypervigilant, they may also be keenly aware of subtle changes in the therapist's facial expression or body language created by countertransference. This is another example of when you as the therapist may need to be open about your own process. Both transference and countertransference can be excellent and informative tools for psychotherapy—if you recognize them for what they are and know how to use them.

If possible, I recommend that you obtain a copy of the Dissociative Experiences Scale (DES), described in

Chapter 4, and take it yourself without minimizing your symptoms. If you score above 12, that's an indication that you have a higher than normal level of dissociation going on and that the symptoms may not be sufficiently under control. Depending on your personal history and the specific items that you endorse, you may be particularly vulnerable to being triggered while doing trauma work. It would be a good idea to seek out therapy to deal with your own trauma-related symptoms before taking on dissociative clients.

Beyond recognizing your own unresolved problems and being committed to working on them, there's the issue of self-care. Your patients can't be healthier than you are. Take vacations, cultivate friendships, read good books, laugh often. Eat properly, get enough sleep, and make time for exercise. Think of all the positive, healthy things you recommend to your patients and take your own advice.

Another aspect of this work is that you have to be prepared to listen to, and be fully present with, recollections that are almost literally unspeakable and feelings that are gut-wrenching. Even the more typical, "garden variety" child abuse may include soul-searing stories of physical, emotional and sexual abuse and profound neglect and rejection at the hands of family members, neighbors, coaches, clergy persons, and so on. Beyond that, some patients will bring you their stories of torture, murder and other horrors. Therapists doing deep trauma work run a very real risk of vicarious PTSD—that is, of being traumatized themselves by what they hear from patients. Some therapists respond to this experience by going into denial. They find that they can't allow themselves to believe that such things really happen in their own communities. They shouldn't be doing deep trauma work. Other therapists respond to this experience by rushing in as rescuers. They shouldn't be doing deep trauma work, either, at least until they have more of their own traumas resolved. For the rest of us, paying attention to excellent personal and professional self-care is essential. Good trauma therapists have skilled peers they can consult with, strong psycho-social support networks — and good therapists of their own, when needed.

Adults who were abused as children often have markedly poor boundaries — either too rigid or too porous, or some of both. It's essential, therefore, that the therapist be constantly mindful of clear, consistent, appropriate boundaries. Trauma, especially in the form of abuse, can be thought of as a boundary violation. Child abuse survivors have been violated, often in every possible way, so they don't know what good, healthy boundaries feel like. Sometimes they will pull for the therapist to cross a boundary — because that's what feels normal, expected and understandable to them, or perhaps because they're testing you to see if you'll behave like the abusers. At some point, you'll almost certainly be tempted to strike up a friendship, lend a patient money, take her home with you, etc. But part of your job is to be very clear about where your healthy boundaries are and gently but firmly stick to them.

On the other hand, as important as it is to be consistent with boundaries and limits, it's equally important to pay attention to what's happening when the limits are being tested, because protectors will sometimes try to use them against you. For example, if the patient is chronically late by 5 or 10 minutes, it may be the protectors' way of cutting down her time with you. If you have a rule that a patient who is late loses any missed time, and you stick to it in this case, you'll be inadvertently reinforcing the protectors' negative behavior. One creative solution, from a colleague of mine (Beaudoin, 2007), is to note how many minutes the patient is late, double it, and tack the time onto the end of the session. This approach effectively foils the protectors' intentions. However, note that this solution would *not* be appropriate for, say, a non-DID patient whose chronic tardiness was caused by poor time management. In that case, it would have the opposite effect—giving the extra time would reward the undesirable behavior.

It helps in this kind of work to be a little obsessive-compulsive. Details are important. For example, this may seem obvious to some readers, but if you're working with an abuse survivor, it's essential for you to show up for every appointment and to show up on time. If this patient is your first of the day, you need to be there early enough that your patient doesn't arrive to find a locked door. Other small details might include adjusting the lighting or making sure that there's hot water for tea. With some patients, you might even want to let them know when you're planning to change your hairstyle (or anything else that would abruptly alter your appearance, or the appearance of your office).

It's also important to be precise in your use of language, because some parts and aspects will take what you say literally. I once made the mistake of saying, after greeting a patient in the waiting room, "I'll be back in a minute." Of course what I meant was "I'll be back in a short while," but that wasn't what I said, nor what she heard. When I came back about five minutes later, the protectors had jumped on it, called me a liar, and gotten the entire system very upset.

It's vital that patients know they can depend on you and your consistency. If you're often late; if you often have to cancel or change appointments, especially on short notice; if you often become defensive or overwhelmed; you'll be proving to the patient that you can't be trusted, any more than the perpetrators could. No matter how long the patient stays in therapy, it's likely that it will ultimately fail. On the other hand, trauma survivors (with the possible exception of those with borderline personality disorder) won't expect you to be perfect. If you make the effort from the very beginning to demonstrate that you're centered and present and that you genuinely care about the patient's comfort, you'll build trust and rapport. For a trauma survivor, that's an excellent new beginning.

The principles above apply to working with any form of severe trauma. If you choose to work with DID, however, there are two other very important cautions. First, don't fall in love with the system. A DID system is an amazingly creative and beautiful construction. It's easy to become entranced with its intricacy and to want to know everything about it — what the parts' names and ages are, who speaks to whom, what they like to do, and so on. The child parts in particular can be quite charming — and the protectors are more than capable of pushing them out front in order to charm and distract you. But that's moving in the wrong direction. If the therapist treats the parts as if they were real, separate people or attaches playful names to their roles, the compliant patient who wants to please her therapist will make the parts more distinct and separate than they were originally, increasing the dissociation.

Second, remember what I said earlier about working with the core. She is the one who ultimately needs to do the work in therapy, not the parts, and she is the only one who has the power to make changes. That doesn't mean that you don't ever talk to the parts—you have to start where the patient is. If the core isn't initially out front, though, it does mean keeping this principle in mind and gently, consistently working to gain the core's trust and her willingness to work with you directly.

A last word. If you do decide to do this work, seek out additional training. Treating severe trauma is a specialty, in the same way that emergency medicine is a specialty. Read widely. Look for whatever continuing education you can find. Arrange for consultation with an experienced practitioner. And most of all, listen to what your patients teach you.

References

American Psychiatric Association (2022). *Diagnostic and statistical manual of mental disorders (DSM-5 TR)* (5th ed., text rev.). American Psychiatric Association Press.

Arenson, G. (2001). *Five simple steps to emotional healing.* Simon and Schuster.

Armstrong, C. (2019). *Rethinking trauma treatment.* W. W. Norton & Company.

Association for Comprehensive Energy Psychology (2022). Quick facts: The science behind energy psychology. Retrieved from www.energypsych.org/ researchdb8c7 1b7#ResearchQuickFacts.

Beaudoin, P. (1998). Personal communication.

Beaudoin, P. (2007). Personal communication.

Becker, R. O. (1985). *The body electric.* William Morrow & Co.

Bernstein, E. M., & Putnam, F. W. (1986). Development, reliability, and validity of a dissociation scale. *The Journal of Nervous and Mental Disease, 174,* 727-735.

Braun, B. G. (1988). The BASK model of dissociation: Part I. *Dissociation, 1,* 4-23.

Brough, K. (1995). Consultation group on the treatment of dissociative disorders, Atlanta, GA.

Brown, D., Scheflin, A. W., & Hammond, C. D. (1998). *Memory, trauma treatment and the law*. W. W. Norton & Company.

Callahan, R. J. (1985). *Five-minute phobia cure: Dr. Callahan's treatment for fear, phobias and self-sabotage*. Enterprise Publishing, Inc.

Callahan, R. J. (2000). *Tapping the healer within*. McGraw-Hill.

Carlson, E.B. & Putnam, F.W. (1993). An update on the Dissociative Experience Scale. *Dissociation 6*(1), 16-27.

Carrington, P. (2001). *How to create positive choices in energy psychology: The Choices training manual*. Pace Educational Systems.

Church, D. (2016). Consciousness as an epigenetic intervention. Presented at the Eighteenth Annual Conference of the Association for Comprehensive Energy Psychology, Santa Clara, CA.

Church, D. (2018). *Mind over matter: The astonishing science of how your brain creates material reality*. Hay House, Inc.

Clinton, A. N. (2006). *Seemorg Matrix Work: The basics*. Seemorg LLC.

Craig, G. (1999). *Emotional freedom techniques: The manual (3rd ed.)*. El Paso: Mediacopy. Also available at www.emofree.com.

Dana, D. (2018). *The Polyvagal Theory in therapy*. W. W. Norton & Company.

de Becker, G. (1999). *The gift of fear and other survival signals that protect us from violence*. Dell.

De Waal, F. (2012). Moral behavior in animals. TED talk, April, 2012. Retrieved from https://www.ted.com/speakers/frans_de_waal.

Dillon, J. (2001). What children can teach adults about spirituality. Talk given at UUMAN, Roswell, GA.

Dorahy, M. J., Brand, B. L., Sar, V., Kruger, C., Stavropoulos, P., Martinez-Taboas, A., Lewis-Fernandez, R., & Middleton, W. (2014). Dissociative identity disorder: An empirical overview. Australian & New Zealand Journal of Psychiatry, 48(5), 402-417. doi.org/10.1177/0004867414527523

Feinstein, D. (2019). Energy psychology: Efficacy, speed, mechanisms. Explore, 15(5), 340-351. doi:10.1016/j.explore.2018.11.003

Felitti, V. J., Anda, R. F., Nordenberg, D., Williamson, D. F., Spitz, A. M., Edwards, V., Koss, M. P., & Marks, J. S. (1998). Relationship of childhood abuse and household dysfunction to many of the leading causes of death in adults. The Adverse Childhood Experiences (ACE) Study. American Journal of Preventive Medicine, 14(4), 245-258. doi: 10.1016/s0749-3797(98)00017-8.

Florida Vedic College (2001). History. www.floridavediccollege.edu/frame_arts.htm.

Fung, P. C. W. (2009). Probing the mystery of Chinese medicine meridian channels with special emphasis on the connective tissue interstitial fluid system, mechanotransduction, cells durotaxis and mast cell degranulation. Chinese Medicine, 4(1), 1-6.

Eldringhoff, S. (2014). Personal communication.

Gallo, F. P. (2000). *Energy diagnostic and treatment methods.* W. W. Norton.

Herman, J. L. (1992). *Trauma and recovery.* Basic.

Hover-Kramer, D. (2002). *Healing touch: Guidebook for practitioners.* Delmar/Thomson International.

International Center for Reiki Training (2007). www.reiki. org/FAQ/HistoryOfReiki/html.

Jang, K. L., Paris, J., Zweig-Frank, H., & Livesley, W. J. (1998). Twin study of dissociative experience. *Journal of Nervous and Mental Disease, 186*(6), 345-351. doi. org/10.1097/00005053-199806000-00004

Jones, C. D. (1974). Personal communication.

Karjala, L. M. (1999). Treatment of acute trauma. Presented (with Pati Beaudoin, Ed.D.) at the Advanced Hypnosis Workshop, American Society of Clinical Hypnosis, Atlanta, GA.

Karjala, L. M. (2022). *Healing everyday traumas: Free yourself from the scars of bullying, criticism and other old wounds.* Psychology Innovations Press.

Katherine, A. (1991). *Boundaries: Where you end and I begin.* Parkside Publishing.

Katherine, A. (2000). *Where to draw the line: How to set healthy boundaries every day.* Fireside.

Kramer, P. (1993). *Listening to Prozac.* Penguin.

Krieger, D. (1979). *Therapeutic touch.* Prentice Hall.

Langevin, H. M. & Yandow, J. A. (2002). Relationship of acupuncture points and meridians to connective tissue planes. *Anatomical Record, 269*(6), 257–265.

Levine, P. A. (2018). Polyvagal theory and trauma. In S. W. Porges & D. Dana (Eds.), *Clinical applications of the Polyvagal Theory: The emergence of polyvagal-informed therapies.* W. W. Norton & Company.

Linehan, M. (2019). *Skills training manual for treating borderline personality disorder (2nd Ed, Rev.).* New Harbinger Publications.

MacLean, P. (1990). *The triune brain in evolution: Role in paleocerebral functions.* Springer Publishing.

McCarthy,J. (1995). Advanced workshop on M-E abuse. Workshop presented in Atlanta, GA.

McKay, M., & Fanning, P. (2000). *Self-esteem (3rd Ed.).* New Harbinger Publications.

McKinnon, M. C., Boyd, J. E., Frewen, P.A., Lanius, U. F., Jetly, R., Richardson, J. D., & Lanius, R.A. (2016). A review of the relation between dissociation, memory, executive functioning and social cognition in military members and civilians with neuropsychiatric conditions. *Neuropsychologia, 90,* 210-234. doi. org/10.1016/j.neuropsychologia.2016.07.017Mc

Taggart, L. (2008). *The field: The quest for the secret force of the universe.* Harper Perennial.

Oschman, J. L. (2015). *Energy medicine: The scientific basis (2nd Ed.).* Churchill Livingstone.

Page, S. (2013). *Happily married: The 8 essential traits of couples who thrive.* RosettaBooks.

Pert, C.B. (1997). *The molecules of emotion.* Scribner's.

Porges, S. W. (2011a). Somatic perspectives on psychotherapy (S. Prengel, Interviewer). [Transcript] Retrieved from https://static1.squarespace.com/static/ 5c1d025fb27e 390a78569537/t/5cce0263eef1a108d7313ea7/ 1557004900220/serge_prengel_interview.pdf

Porges, S. W. (2011b). The polyvagal theory: Neurophysiological foundations of emotions, attachment, communication, and self-regulation. W. W. Norton.

Porges, S. W. (2018). Polyvagal theory: A primer.. In S. W. Porges & D. Dana (Eds.), *Clinical applications of the Polyvagal Theory: The emergence of polyvagal-informed therapies.* W. W. Norton & Company.

Ross, C. A. (1997). *Dissociative identity disorder.* John Wiley & Sons.

Schore, A. N. (2009). Attachment trauma and the developing right brain: Origins of pathological dissociation (107-141). In Dell, P. F., and O'Neil, J. A. (Eds.), *Dissociation and the dissociative disorders: DSM-V and beyond.* Routledge.

Şar, V. (2011). Epidemiology of dissociative disorders: An overview. *Epidemiology Research International*, 2011, 1–8. doi:10.1155/2011/404538

Schrader, S. (1993). Recent advances in the dissociative disorders: Theory, research and practice. Workshop presented in Atlanta, GA.

Smith, M. J. (1975). *When I say no, I feel guilty: How to cope using the skills of systematic assertiveness therapy.* Bantam Books.

van der Kolk, B. (2014). *The body keeps the score: Brain, mind, and body in the healing of trauma.* Penguin Books.

Wolf, E. J., Rassmusson, A. M., Mitchell, K. S., Logue, M. W.,

Baldwin, C. T., & Miller, M. W. (2014). A genome-wide association study of clinical symptoms of dissociation in a trauma-exposed sample. *Depression and Anxiety, 31*(4), 352-360. doi: 10.1002/da.22260

APPENDIX A

The Science of Trauma

Earlier in the book, I mentioned there used to be a great deal of controversy about the nature of traumatic memory and, in particular, whether traumatic memories are different from "normal" memories. On an experiential level, trauma survivors consistently tell us that traumatic memories *feel* different. They don't feel like long-ago, faraway events, but rather like experiences that are happening right now in the present moment, at full intensity. An increasing body of research shows that the brain and nervous system respond differently to traumatic events and nontraumatic events. Traumatic events trigger responses in the brain and nervous system that don't happen with nontraumatic events. And as we'll see, there is evidence these biochemical and physiological responses may create long-term changes in neuronal pathways in the brain (McKinnon, Boyd, Frewen, Lanius, Jetly, Richardson, & Lanius, 2016), as well as serious consequences for overall health (Dana, 2018).

184 | Understanding Trauma and Dissociation

In this chapter, we'll take a look at both the experiential and scientific ways of understanding trauma. First, we'll review the BASK model (discussed in Chapter 3), which focuses on the experiential differences between traumatic and nontraumatic memory. Then, we'll review some recent scientific findings for a deeper understanding of the effects of trauma on a physical level as well as the psychological impact of those effects.

The BASK Model of Experience

As I explained earlier, this theory suggests that our memory of any experience is made up of four major components that form the acronym BASK (Braun, 1988):

- **B** stands for **behavior**. This includes all of the body movements that we made or witnessed during the experience.

- **A** stands for **affect**, another word for emotion. In a pleasant memory, this might include happiness, joy, excitement and love. In a traumatic experience, it's likely to be fear, anxiety, anger, rage, guilt, shame, hopelessness, or helplessness.

- **S** is for **sensation**, all the sensory information that gets registered during the experience—sights, sounds, smells, pain, etc.

- **K** stands for **knowledge**, the cognitive awareness of what happened, including our interpretations of the event and the beliefs we form about it.

In nontraumatic circumstances, it seems all four components are experienced together and stored together in normal narrative memory. Normal storage is like leaving the memory out in the yard exposed to the elements. Parts of it erode very quickly, especially the sensory information, so when we recall it there's a very clear difference between experiencing it the first time and remembering it afterwards. If I asked you what you had for dinner a couple of nights ago, the odds are you could tell me, but you probably wouldn't be tasting it as you were remembering.

According to the theory, though, traumatic memories are quite different. During a traumatic experience one or more of the components get split off, or dissociated, and stored separately. Instead of being exposed to normal erosion, it's as if a part of the mind becomes frozen in that moment in time and held in the subconscious — much like "Ötzi," the 5,300 year-old man who was found in a glacier in 1991, amazingly well preserved in the ice. Time doesn't seem to matter at all. It certainly does not "heal all wounds." At best, the passage of time may cover up emotional wounds, but when a trauma memory is recalled, it comes back with its full impact. Even decades later, the person feels as if the trauma is happening *now*, not in some distant past.

The Biology of Trauma

Braun's BASK model helps us to relate to the experience of trauma. But our reaction to trauma is not simply thoughts, feelings and beliefs. Trauma creates a *whole-body response*. Looking at the most basic level, the ends of neurons (nerve cells) don't actually touch each other. There's a gap between the end of one neuron and the beginning of the next, called a synapse. A neuron fires by sending an electrical impulse down its length, releasing a chemical message across the synapse that triggers or inhibits the firing of the next neuron. Every thought and feeling we have, every behavior we engage in, has to be manifested in the brain and body in the form of these electrical and biochemical changes. Therefore, it's helpful to understand something about the biology of trauma — as well as how it's experienced on a psychological level — in order to fully understand its effects on how we feel and how we perceive ourselves and the world.

My aim here is to provide you with a basic understanding of the impact of trauma on the body. If you want to know more, there are dozens of books and hundreds of articles available, such as Porges (2011a, 2011b, 2018), van der Kolk (2014) and Rosenberg (2017). One of the best recent books is *Rethinking Trauma Treatment* by Courtney Armstrong (2019), who offers an excellent, readable description of the parts of the brain, what responsibilities they have, and how they communicate with each other. I strongly recommend her first chapter for anyone wanting to learn about this information in greater detail. Deb Dana's (2018) book, *The Polyvagal Theory in Therapy,* is also a great resource for therapists and covers much of the material in this chapter in a therapeutic context.

The Nervous System

It will help to start our exploration of the science of trauma with a brief review of the parts of the nervous system. The human nervous system has two divisions: the **central nervous system**, or CNS (the brain and spinal cord) and the **peripheral nervous system**, or PNS (everything else). In evolutionary terms, we can think of the brain as "triune" — that is, having three main parts. The most ancient part is called the reptilian brain, followed by the mammalian brain and, finally, the cerebral cortex (MacLean, 1990).

- The **reptilian brain** is located at the bottom of the brain, close to the spinal cord. It regulates essential bodily functions and supports our basic, physical survival.

- The **mammalian brain** is located in the center of the skull. It has also been called the "emotional brain." It contains the limbic system, which is involved in emotional reaction and the experience of deep-seated feelings such as pleasure and anger. It affects learning and memory, motivation, attention and time perception.

- The **cerebral cortex** is the outermost layer of the brain. The **prefrontal cortex**, the part just behind the forehead, is involved in such functions as higher-order thinking, logic and reasoning, language, and the conscious regulation and processing of emotion.

188 | Understanding Trauma and Dissociation

The diagram below shows these three parts.

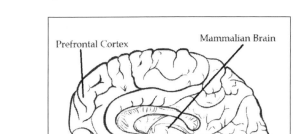

Diagram 4: The Triune Brain

The peripheral nervous system (PNS) in turn has two main parts, the somatic and the autonomic. The **somatic nervous system** controls voluntary movements of the body. The **autonomic nervous system** (ANS) is where we want to turn our attention.

The traditional description of the autonomic nervous system also has two divisions, the parasympathetic system and the sympathetic system. The parasympathetic system produces the **relaxation response**. When the parasympathetic system is in control, we feel calm. We have the capacity to feel alert, interested, and happy. Our heart rate and breathing are normal. Blood is flowing to our digestive system and other internal organs. The prefrontal cortex, the most advanced part of the brain where conscious thinking and decision-making occur, is active and able to exercise good judgment. The parasympathetic system is controlled by the vagus nerve.

In contrast, the sympathetic system produces the **activation response**. This happens when the limbic system in the mammalian part of our brain detects danger cues. The sympathetic system causes us to startle for a tiny fraction of a second. But it's long enough release a spurt of adrenaline, and we become hyperalert. If the threat turns out to be nothing — a shadow on the wall, for example, and not an attacker — the normal reaction is to return to a regulated, parasympathetic state. If the perception of threat continues, on the other hand, the sympathetic system triggers what we know as the fight/ flight response. Our whole body gears up to either fight or flee (Dana, 2018). Our heart rate and breathing speed up. Cortisol is released and causes blood flow to be rerouted from the internal organs to the large muscles of the arms and legs. One of the more unfortunate changes is that blood flow to the higher thinking centers of the brain is also reduced (Church, 2016). We respond reflexively, without rational thought. This makes sense from an evolutionary viewpoint — if a saber tooth tiger is charging at you, and you have to stop and reason out what your response should be, you're already done for. But it helps us understand why terror is sometimes described as "mindless" or "unreasoning." Here's another example:

> *When Beth was 10, she got to go to summer camp for a whole month. She got along well with her cabin mates and loved all of the activities. Toward the end of the term, there was a huge campfire celebration for*

the entire camp, and her cabin was assigned the task of gathering firewood. Unfortunately, someone stirred up a yellow jacket nest, and several people – including Beth – were painfully stung. Over the next few days, Beth found herself flinching when she heard any kind of buzzing sound. One afternoon, while she and her bunkmates were waiting outside of their cabin, a big bumblebee flew toward her and started circling her. She was terrified. Her vision went black, and she felt completely frozen. She was dimly aware of the sound of screams. When it finally flew away – probably within seconds, though it felt like an hour – she realized that she was the one who was screaming.

Other areas of the brain necessary for the integration of incoming information (including the hippocampus and the thalamus) are also disconnected, preventing memories from being stored in an organized and coherent way (van der Kolk, 2014). Armstrong (2019) went into this point in greater detail. She explained that the part of the limbic system called the amygdala is responsible for encoding the experiential components of an event into *implicit memory*, which includes behavioral impulses, emotions and sensory impressions. (Note that the experiential components listed by Armstrong parallel the B, A and S components described in Braun's [1988] BASK theory.)

An implicit memory is a kind of mental model or diagram that the amygdala will use in the future in its job as our brain's threat detector. Under conditions that are not particularly stressful, the thalamus and hippocampus (in the limbic system) and the prefrontal cortex stay connected to this process and are able to add contextual details to the amygdala's mental model to create an *explicit memory*. The explicit memory of the event includes the factual details and our understanding of where the event fits into our personal history and what meaning it holds for us (roughly parallel to Braun's K component).

Under severe stress, however, when cortisol and endogenous opioids are being released, the brain's ability to form explicit memories is impaired. "Thus, the sensory cues associated with the traumatic experience stay locked in implicit memory and fail to be integrated with the context and knowledge contained in higher cortical regions" (Armstrong, 2019, p. 31). This finding supports Braun's idea that some of the components of a traumatic memory are dissociated and stored separately—specifically, according to Armstrong, the behavior, affect, and sensory components from the cognitive component.

Porges' Polyvagal Theory

In the past, people often referred to the fight/flight response as "fight/flight/freeze." Thanks to the brilliant work of Steven Porges (2011b, 2018), however, we now understand that the freeze response is a completely different event and comes from a different part of the brain. In the 1990s, when Porges was a researcher at the University of Maryland studying heart rate patterns in human fetuses and newborns, he began to notice a strange phenomenon: the parasympathetic system could trigger brachycardia, a slowing of the heart rate so severe it can actually be fatal.

How was it that the parasympathetic system, which is usually associated with relaxation and resilience, instead put the organism in significant danger?

The answer, Porges discovered, is that there are two branches of the vagus nerve that act in quite different ways. We now refer to this finding as his **polyvagal theory**. The ventral (front) vagal nerve is the one associated with the classic parasympathetic response that we've already described. Among other things, it's linked to cranial nerves connected to the eyes, the middle ear, and muscles of the face. It allows us to tune in to calm facial expressions and the tonal qualities of soothing speech. Porges called this the *social engagement system*. Our first inclination when alerted, then, is to turn to our pack, family or tribe. We feel more secure when we can turn to a supportive person — or even better, a group — whom we perceive as safe.

Sometimes, though, the social engagement system isn't available. In an emergency, there may literally be no one else around to help. Even without a crisis situation, we may feel isolated, with no one we feel we can turn to. Worse, because of a history of prior trauma, we may not view *any* other person as safe. Or the threat may be to the whole group, so that safety isn't assured even with our pack around us. In those situations, the second line of defense is *mobilization* — the activation of the sympathetic nervous system and the fight/flight response.

But what if we can't fight or escape? Porges discovered there's a second branch of the vagus, the dorsal (back) vagal nerve, that operates differently. When mobilization is impossible or ineffective, and the danger is perceived as life-threatening, the dorsal vagal nerve triggers *immobilization,* a response that comes from the much more ancient and primitive reptilian brain. Heart rate and respiration slow, as they do when the normal relaxation response of the parasympathetic system is triggered. In this case, however, they may decrease to dangerously low levels (Porges, 2018) and cause the organism to freeze in place or even to lose consciousness. Colloquially, we often refer to this response as "playing possum" or "playing dead," but it's anything but play. It's more appropriately called "death feigning" or thanatosis. (Some writers have differentiated between "freeze," when the organism is conscious but immobilized, and "faint," when the organism becomes unconscious. Porges includes both of these responses in the same category, triggered by the dorsal vagal nerve.)

It's easy to see how this category of response might be life-saving for a young animal in the wild. In contrast to the fight/flight response, which rapidly drains metabolic resources, the energy resources of the organism are conserved. Any kind of sound or movement might attract a predator, even breathing or heartbeat, so it's safer to stay absolutely silent. Moreover, many predators won't eat dead carcasses and may pass by an animal that looks dead, even if they do detect its presence.

In human beings, however, this kind of parasympathetic response can be maladaptive, even catastrophic. In the immediate moment of a trauma, we may indeed become physically and mentally frozen, unable to move or speak or think. The emotional shock may cause us to faint. In the early aftermath, we may not remain completely immobilized, but our muscles may be limp, and it can feel as if we're trying to move through thick mud or quicksand. It may be difficult to speak clearly or to describe the experience in words. We may feel numb, hopeless, helpless, and apathetic.

A significant part of the body's response to trauma is the release of endorphins and other endogenous opioids to protect against pain. For the most part, this is a highly adaptive mechanism in helping us to survive the event. As we've discussed, however, these substances also interfere with the creation of integrated, explicit memories. As such, they're a key biochemical component in what causes dissociation and difficulty in remembering a trauma. Beth's experience, described above, illustrates some of these reactions.

Levine (2018) pointed to another finding about thanatosis in animals that may further add to our understanding of the effects of trauma on humans. He noted that most wild animals recover from thanatosis within minutes. If the animal is restrained, however, and is frightened *before* or *during* the restraint, it not only goes into thanatosis but remains frozen in that state for much longer. I find myself wondering if that phenomenon might sometimes happen in a more subtle way — i.e., if even a relatively minor restraint as a component of a trauma might cause more lingering symptoms of the freeze response.

The Concept of Hierarchy

One aspect to note about polyvagal theory is that these three types of responses are arranged in a hierarchy, from the newest and most advanced (in evolutionary terms) to the oldest and most primitive. Our natural tendency is to turn to the highest response first, and only if it fails to provide safety do we move to the next step down the ladder. Even more than that, though, Porges (2018) maintained that the higher neurological structures and processes actually inhibit the lower ones. By extension, this observation suggests that if we're fully ensconced in the social engagement system, we may be less likely to go into the sympathetic activation of a fight/flight state — or at least may do so more slowly.

As a side note, it's interesting to remember that this concept of hierarchy applies on a psychological level as well. Since Sigmund Freud started writing about defense mechanisms in the 1890s, it's been observed that we typically rely on our most sophisticated behaviors and coping mechanisms first. If they don't get us what we want or don't work to relieve our anxiety, though, we tend to regress to younger, less mature behavior patterns or ways of coping — such as throwing a temper tantrum. This tendency can also be observed when we're under ongoing forms of stress. How often have you noticed that, when someone is in bed with even a mild illness, they crave the kinds of things that were comforting to them as children? (And sometimes behave like children if they don't get them?)

Porges' concepts of hierarchy and inhibition also shed light on the concept of "reciprocal inhibition," coined by psychiatrist Joseph Wolpe in the 1950s. Wolpe reasoned that a person couldn't feel anxious and non-anxious at the same time. He applied this observation in creating the technique he named "systematic desensitization." This technique is still in use today, especially as a treatment for phobias (and it's the principle behind the Healing Room described in Chapter 10). In a classic desensitization approach, the patient is first taught a relaxation technique, such as diaphragmatic breathing. Once that's mastered, the patient begins a slow approach to the feared object or situation until the fear response is extinguished. The approach can be done in imagination or *in vivo* — i.e., in real life.

For example, let's say a therapist is working with a man who has a phobia of mice. After teaching him a relaxation technique, the therapist has him stand in the doorway of a room that has a mouse in a cage at the far end. She instructs the man to enter the room and approach the cage until he begins to feel the fear. At that point, she has the man stop and practice relaxation until the fear ebbs. If necessary, he may back away. As they continue working, over many trials (and usually several sessions), the man becomes able to move closer and closer to the cage until he can stand over it and look at the mouse without fear. He may even get to the point of being able to touch or handle the mouse comfortably.

We can now understand what's happening with this technique on a physiological level. The relaxation technique triggers the parasympathetic system, which then takes control and quiets the sympathetic system's response to the fear stimulus. Over time, the previously feared object is no longer interpreted as a threat by the limbic system in the emotional brain. We talked about the use of controlled breathing as a relaxation technique in Chapter 13. It's actually possible to apply systematic desensitization techniques to yourself without a therapist, especially if the phobia is a minor one. However, I think Porges would add that the presence of another person who gives what he calls "neuroceptive" cues of safety and calm also helps to elicit the social engagement system and further inhibit the fight/flight response.

Neuroception

Returning to polyvagal theory, another aspect to highlight is that the social engagement, fight/flight and freeze states are triggered at a subconscious level. We don't enter them by reasoned decision, or even by conscious choice. Sensory information, including information about possible threat, goes first to the thalamus and is then sent on to both the amygdala and the frontal lobes. However, the pathway to the amygdala is much faster than the one to the higher centers of the brain, and we may react before we think (van der Kolk, 2014). Porges uses the term "neuroception" to distinguish this process from conscious perception. He describes neuroception as "a reflexive mechanism capable of instantaneously shifting physiological state" (2018, p. 58). This detection system is capable not only of observing cues such as body movements, hand gestures and facial expressions but also of interpreting their intention. For example, a raised fist accompanied by an angry facial expression will be recognized as a threat, even if the fist isn't yet moving toward you. In contrast, a raised fist accompanied by an exultant facial expression is more likely to be interpreted as a celebration of victory (and, if it's your team, may enhance the social engagement response).

The phenomenon of neuroception may help explain many of the instances in which we react emotionally to a person or a situation without knowing why. At times, it may be we're accurately picking up on the kind of subconscious danger cues that de Becker (1999) described in *The Gift of Fear*. Perhaps the emotional brain is noticing an edge to the voice or a narrowing of the eyes that tells us this person may be shifty and untrustworthy. It's also possible, though, that the cues picked up by the amygdala only *resemble* details from a previous trauma. In that case, we feel threatened when there's no actual danger in the present day. For example, one of my patients struggled all through third grade — dissociated and inattentive — because she was afraid of her teacher. Years later, she made the connection that the teacher looked like her abusive aunt, and she realized the sense of danger had come from a different time and place.

Long-Term Effects of Trauma and Stress

The review by McKinnon et al. (2016) cited substantial evidence that dissociation associated with trauma-related disorders has been linked to a wide variety of neurological and cognitive impairments in such functions as attention and episodic and autobiographical memory. Deficits may be seen in all areas of executive functioning, including planning, initiating, and prioritizing activities; maintaining emotional regulation and impulse control; self-motivation; and self-awareness. Notably, these kinds of deficits have been found not only in the immediate aftermath of a trauma, but also in adults who had experienced abuse or neglect in childhood. In other words, there is reason to be concerned that these negative changes are long-term and perhaps permanent.

In discussing the functioning of the autonomic nervous system, Dana (2018) made an intriguing comment:

A working principle of the autonomic nervous system is 'every response is an action in service of survival.' No matter how incongruous an action may look from the outside, from an autonomic perspective it is always an adaptive survival response. The autonomic nervous system doesn't make a judgment about good and bad; it simply acts to manage risk and seek safety (p. 6).

When the sympathetic system is chronically activated, however, the effects may be debilitating. For a person who is already traumatized, a new stressor causes the stress hormones to spike more quickly, to reach higher levels, and to return to baseline more slowly (van der Kolk, 2014). The result is often significant psychological problems, such as generalized anxiety, panic attacks, aggression, irritability and anger issues (Armstrong, 2019). The more intense and longer-lasting autonomic responses make it harder for people to remain in a calm, regulated state, and their relationships may suffer because of their chronic feelings of unsafety. Over time, elevated cortisol may also contribute to long-term problems with physical health, including high blood pressure and heart disease, sleep difficulties, muscle tightness, digestive problems, and decreased immune function (Dana, 2018).

Dana further noted that, although these early survival responses are originally beneficial, they may become habitual and maladaptive. As a result, the world may come to be seen as "dangerous, chaotic, and unfriendly" (Dana, 2018, p. 11).

The elevated levels of cortisol and adrenaline caused by trauma and stress also have significant negative effects on physical health. The original study of the effects of adverse childhood experiences showed a strong connection with several of the leading causes of death, including heart disease, cancer, chronic lung disease and liver disease (Felitti, Anda, Nordenberg, Williamson, Spitz, Edwards, Koss & Marks, 1998). In my own practice, I've noticed that virtually every one of my patients with a history of severe childhood abuse has at least one form of chronic illness, such as multiple sclerosis or congestive heart failure. Church (2016) offered a possible explanation for this connection. He suggested that a chronically increased cortisol level undermines the functioning of our immune system by depleting the body of a particular hormone. Dehydroepiandrosterone (DHEA) is a hormone essential for cell communication, repair and regeneration. DHEA and cortisol are made from the same chemicals in the body. The body doesn't keep great stockpiles of these chemicals, so when it needs more cortisol, it breaks down DHEA to get them. If the heightened demand for cortisol continues, so does the relative deficiency of DHEA. Church maintained that reduced DHEA contributes to reduced bone and skin cell repair, accelerated aging, slower wound healing, decreased circulating immune cells, diminished immune antibodies, death of brain cells, and reduced muscle mass, among other things.

Trauma and Dissociation

Dana (2018) went on to describe the consequences of long-term activation of the dorsal vagal parasympathetic response. If the immediate "deer in headlights" freeze response becomes chronic, the feelings of numbness, hopelessness and apathy may become an ingrained pattern. We may experience depression and memory problems. The consequences to physical health may include chronic fatigue, fibromyalgia, type 2 diabetes, or various types of autoimmune disease (Dana, 2018; van der Kolk, 2014).

A similar point can be made about chronic dissociation. Schore (2009) noted that a typical (i.e., not highly traumatized) person initially uses dissociation as an adaptive coping mechanism for dealing with significantly traumatic events. Over time, however, the dissociation may become habitual. It begins to be used for a wider and wider range of stressors, large and small—including the person's own PTSD symptoms, which by this time have become stressors in their own right. Schore further noted that "this psychic-deadening defense is maladaptive not only because the individual resorts to dissociation at low levels of stress, but also finds it difficult to exit this state" (2009, p. 115).

In his influential work *The Body Keeps the Score*, van der Kolk (2014) noted that dissociation is the "essence" of trauma. Recall that even without our current knowledge about the underlying physiology, Braun (1988) observed that trauma is not stored in normal narrative memory. He pointed out that a trauma memory seems to be splintered into its component parts and those components stored separately. Years later, van der Kolk agreed that "the overwhelming experience is split off and fragmented, so that the emotions, sounds, images, thoughts, and physical sensations related to the trauma take on a life of their own" (2014, p. 66). And now we know much more about how and why that happens. As we discussed earlier, when the limbic system detects threat, a cascade of hormones is released, the major thinking centers of the prefrontal cortex are deprived of blood flow, executive functioning is impaired, and the emotional brain takes over. As a result, the cognitive understanding of the event and the ability to describe it verbally (Braun's K component) are dissociated from the emotional and sensory imprints.

In Chapter 2, I mentioned that the capacity for dissociation appears to be inborn and that everyone has some degree of dissociative ability. Evidence now shows that genetics influences the level of a person's dissociative talent (Dorahy, Brand, Sar, Kruger, Stavropoulos, Martinez-Taboas, Lewis-Fernandez, & Middleton, 2014; Jang, Paris, Zweig-Frank, & Livesley, 1998; Wolf, Rassmusson, Mitchell, Logue, Baldwin, & Miller, 2014). These findings help confirm anecdotal observations reported over several decades that dissociative disorders tend to run in families.

Dissociative *disorders* are not inherited as such. Like any other talent, it's not enough to have the ability — the skill must also be practiced in order to develop to its fullest. Repeated childhood trauma appears to provide more than sufficient "practice" of the skill of dissociation. And we can imagine that growing up in a household in which one or more family members have undiagnosed and untreated dissociative disorders could be chaotic, to say the least.

Back to the Experience of Trauma

To go back to our original metaphor: because the traumatic memory is "frozen," it's not subject to normal erosion or weathering. It remains fragmented and isn't integrated with explicit memory. As a result, it has much the full impact of the original event when it gets recalled to conscious awareness. It feels as if we're reliving it, not just remembering it. The feelings, thoughts and beliefs — and sometimes body sensations — can be as clear and vivid as the first time they happened, even if that day was decades before. Even though some or all of the components of the memories are dissociated and we may not be able to recall them on a conscious level, they can and do still exert insidious effects on our present-day behavior and experiences.

About the Author

Dr. Lynn Mary Karjala is a licensed psychologist in private practice in Roswell, Georgia. In addition to her general practice, she has specialized training and extensive clinical experience in the treatment of trauma in all its forms. She also trains other clinicians in the use of both conventional and innovative approaches to therapy and has given many presentations on these topics in the U.S., the U.K., and Canada. Before going into clinical practice, she was a university professor, teaching graduate and undergraduate courses on child, adolescent, and life-span development and the psychology of death and dying. She lives in Roswell with her husband of 38 years and assorted dogs and cats.

Thanks for reading my book!

One of the most rewarding things about writing is building a relationship with my readers. Your opinion and feedback matter to me, so feel free to reach out to me at Lynn@karjala.com. I'd love to know what you think.

If you've enjoyed this book...

Help others discover *Understanding Trauma and Dissociation* by leaving your honest review online. The best support an author can ask for is enthusiastic, word-of-mouth recommendations from satisfied readers.

Would you like to have a recording of the Quintessential Safe Place in the author's own voice? It's available at www.karjala.com/courses for a nominal charge.

Made in United States
Troutdale, OR
10/10/2023

13606118R00122